Better IEPs

How to Develop Legally Correct and Educationally Useful Programs

3rd Edition

by

Barbara D. Bateman, Ph.D., J.D.
&
Mary Anne Linden, M.S., J.D.

03   02   01   00   6   5   4   3

ISBN #1-57035-164-3

Text design by Susan Fogo
Text layout by Venture Publishing
Cover design by Londerville Design

Published and Distributed by:

Sopris West
*Helping You Meet the Needs
of At-Risk Students*

4093 Specialty Place • Longmont, Colorado 80504 • (303) 651-2829
www.sopriswest.com

Dedications and Acknowledgments

This book is dedicated to my parents who celebrated their 60th anniversary in August, 1992. Every day of my life they have modeled what caring about children really means. Perhaps this book will help other parents and teachers as they care about the more than four million children in this country who have IEPs.

The author's sincere thanks to David Chard, whose competence, caring, and energy immeasurably helped this book happen.

—Barbara Bateman

To Barb, without whose inspiration I would never have returned to law school.

and

To Jeremy, who encourages me always to hold tight to my ideals.

—Mary Anne Linden

Barbara D. Bateman, Ph.D., J.D., is a nationally recognized leader in special education law. Dr. Bateman, in collaboration with Dr. Samuel Kirk, helped to distinguish the category of learning disabilities in the 1960s and to develop the special services that would later serve this population. She has four decades of experience as an educator, author, and researcher, and has written more than 100 books, monographs, book chapters, and articles on special education and legal issues. Dr. Bateman has long been associated with the Learning Disabilities Association (LDA), and has served as an advocate for parents of children receiving special education services, representing them in due process hearings and as a consultant. Dr. Bateman is professor emeritus of special education at the University of Oregon, Eugene. Dr. Bateman has consulted with and assisted school districts, state departments, and individuals in all 50 states.

Mary Anne Linden, M.S., J.D., has been a special educator for ten years. She is currently completing a Ph.D. in educational policy and management at the University of Oregon, where she has also been involved in special education teacher training. Her research activities have focused on disability law, special education law, special education practice and reform, and parental involvement in schooling.

Table of Contents

Introduction

The purpose of this book is to give special educators, regular educators, and parents the confidence and know-how to develop Individualized Education Programs, or IEPs, which are both legally correct and educationally useful. Currently, many IEPs are neither.

The IEP process is the centerpiece, the heart and soul, of the Individuals with Disabilities Education Act (IDEA). It is the procedure for devising the "free appropriate public education" (FAPE) to which every eligible child who has a disability and needs special education is entitled. In this book, we explain the role of the IEP in the larger context of the IDEA, and we present a child-centered three-step IEP process.

Chapter One highlights the five main components of the IDEA (Part B). We explain the sequential and interdependent relationships of evaluation, IEP development, and placement. We also briefly review the IDEA's funding and due process provisions, which protect the rights of children and their families and govern dispute resolution.

Chapter Two takes a close look at the law. We answer the most fundamental questions about how to prepare a squeaky clean, legally correct IEP: **Who** develops it? **How** does the IEP team operate? **When** must the IEP team convene? **Where** does the IEP meeting happen? **Why** must IEPs be written? **What** must the IEP contain?

Chapter Three explains how not to develop IEPs. We dissect real-world examples of flawed IEPs and identify several common errors in IEP process and content.

Chapter Four describes a better way. We present the "Non-Form" and explain how to create an educationally useful IEP. We focus particular attention on the three step IEP development process, illustrating each step with examples.

Chapter Five tackles some troublesome issues that have plagued schools since the IDEA was first enacted. We look at judicial decisions and agency rulings that elaborate and clarify these issues.

Four appendices present reference materials to guide school personnel and parents and help them to create correct and useful IEPs: (A) the IDEA statute; (B) IDEA regulations; (C) an appendix to the regulations which interprets, in question and answer format, the requirements of IDEA; and (D) model notification to parents of their rights under the IDEA.

The IDEA Amendments of 1997 became law in July of that year, except for IEP requirements, which take effect July 1, 1998. In order to make this book available to readers as soon as possible, we have based the material on the statute and on the proposed regulations issued in October 1997. We believe the final regulations scheduled for release in April 1998 will not differ materially from the statute and proposed regulations. Therefore, the references to 34 CFR 300 point to the proposed regulations. We also assume the bulk of agency rulings, case law, and Appendix C of the old IDEA regulations continue to offer correct and valid interpretations of the law. Of course, we have excluded any material from cases and rulings and from earlier editions of this book that are inconsistent with the 1997 Amendments.

A well-designed IEP can change a child's schooling experience from one of repeated failure, loss of self-esteem, and limited options to one of achievement, direction, and productivity. Alas, our experiences persuade us that legally correct and educationally useful IEPs are all too rare. We devoutly hope and sincerely believe this book can help change that situation.

The IEP in Perspective

Overview

Since 1977, every child in the United States who has a disability and needs special education has been entitled to a free appropriate public education (FAPE) under a Federal law that is now called the Individuals with Disabilities Education Act (IDEA).

In 1997, Congress amended the IDEA with the intention of:

- Strengthening the role of parents;

- Ensuring access to the general education curriculum and reforms;

- Focusing on teaching and learning while reducing unnecessary paperwork requirements;

- Assisting educational agencies in reducing the costs of improving special education and related services to children with disabilities;

- Increasing accommodation of racial, ethnic, and linguistic diversity to prevent inappropriate identification and labeling;

- Ensuring schools are safe and conducive to learning; and

- Encouraging parents and educators to work out their differences by using nonadversarial dispute resolution (Senate Committee on Labor and Human Resources, 1997).

The IDEA (Part B) has five major components: (1) Evaluation and Identification, (2) Individualized Education Program and Related Services, (3) Placement, (4) Funding, and (5) Procedural Safeguards.

The heart of the IDEA is the Individualized Education Program (IEP). The centrality of the IEP is apparent in many ways. The **Evaluation and Identification** provisions determine who is eligible to have an IEP and contribute to understanding the unique needs of each child, which form the basis of the IEP. The **Placement** component calls for case-by-case placement decisions, based on a child's completed IEP. The **Funding** requirements guarantee a **free** appropriate public education, placing squarely upon school districts (or states) the financial burden of determining eligibility and providing IEPs to children with disabilities. Finally, the **Procedural Safeguards** create a safety net for children and their parents. They are designed to ensure the development and provision of appropriate IEPs, to place parents and the school districts on a level playing field, and to facilitate dispute avoidance or resolution.

In order to appreciate the role of the IEP, it is helpful to diagram the primary components in the sequence in which they affect a student (see Figure 1).

Figure 1

The Right Way

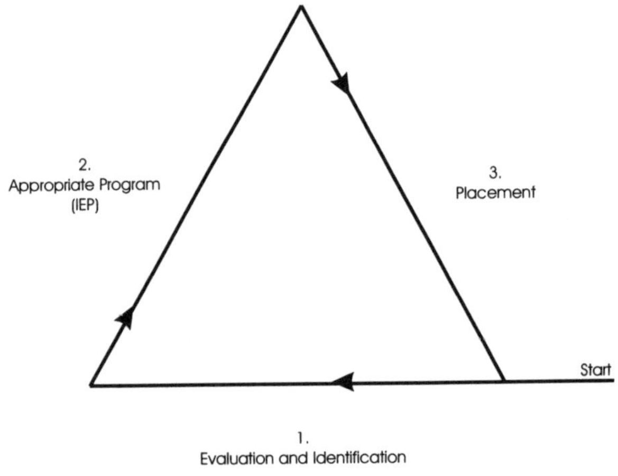

2.
Appropriate Program
(IEP)

3.
Placement

Start

1.
Evaluation and Identification

The first step of the process involves evaluation of a child and a decision on eligibility for FAPE. The second step is the development of an IEP based upon the child's unique needs. The third step is the determination of an appropriate placement based upon the IEP. Reordering of this sequence violates the letter and intent of the IDEA.

The following sections of this chapter include brief descriptions of the five components of the IDEA. Each section ends with "Do's and Don'ts" in the form of advice to those wanting to employ practices that are both legally correct and educationally sound.

Evaluation and Identification

The purposes of the evaluation and identification provisions of the law are to gather functional and developmental information necessary to determine whether a child has one of the disabilities defined in the IDEA, whether the child needs special education and related services, and the child's present levels of performance and individual educational needs (20 U.S.C. §1414).

Evaluation must cover all areas related to a child's suspected disability, including, if appropriate, health, vision, hearing, social and emotional status, general intelligence, academic performance, communication needs, and motor abilities.

The IDEA specifies who participates in the evaluation process. First, the child's IEP team, including the parents, and "other qualified professionals" review existing evaluation data and decide what additional data are needed. The district then administers any needed tests and conducts other evaluation procedures. Finally, "a team of qualified professionals and the parent" makes an eligibility determination. The IDEA regulations explain that "qualified professionals" take part:

> … to ensure that the teams making these determinations include individuals with the knowledge and skills necessary to interpret the evaluation data and make an informed determination as to whether the child is a child with a disability … and to determine whether the child needs special education and related services. The composition of the team will vary depending upon the nature of the child's disability and other relevant factors. For example, if a student is suspected of having a learning disability, a professional whose sole expertise is visual impairments would be an inappropriate choice (34 CFR §300.533 note).

When the suspected disability is specific learning disability (SLD), the eligibility decision is made by:

> ... the child's parents and a team of qualified professionals which must include—
> (a)(1) The child's regular teacher; or (2) If the child does not have a regular teacher, a regular classroom teacher qualified to teach a child of his or her age; or (3) For a child of less than school age, an individual qualified by the SEA to teach a child of his or her age; and (b) At least one person qualified to conduct individual diagnostic examinations of children, such as a school psychologist, speech-language pathologist, or remedial reading teacher (34 CFR 300.540).

The requirements of the law related to evaluation and identification are many (see Figure 2). Some fit well with common school practices, and some do not.

Figure 2

Evaluation and Identification

Ground Rules for Evaluation
from Federal Regulations 34 CFR Part 300

1. Student is referred for evaluation OR student needs reevaluation because:
   - "Conditions warrant" it
   - Parents or teacher have requested it

2. IEP team and "other qualified professionals"*:
   - Review existing evaluation data on the student, including:
     - Information from parents
     - Current classroom-based assessment
     - Observation data from teachers and related service personnel
   - Decide what additional data, if any, is needed to determine:
     - Whether the student has or continues to have an IDEA qualifying disability
     - Student's present levels of performance
     - Whether student needs special education and related services
     - Whether student needs additions or modifications to the special education in order to:
       - Achieve annual goals
       - Participate, as appropriate, in the general curriculum

Standardized tests must:
- Be **validated** for the purpose for which they are used
- Be administered by **trained persons** and in accordance with instructions

Student must be assessed in **all areas** related to suspected disability.

Evaluation may **not** focus solely on IQ, but must assess specific areas of educational need.

Assessment methods must **not discriminate** on the basis of:
- Race
- Culture
- Native language

Evaluation team must use a variety of assessment tools and strategies to:
- **Identify disability**
- **Determine content of IEP**, including information related to enabling student to participate in the general curriculum

No single procedure may be the sole criterion in determining:
- Whether a student has a disability
- A student's appropriate educational program

Tests administered to students with impaired sensory, manual, or speaking skills must accurately **reflect aptitude and ability** rather than reflecting the impairment

Assessment instruments must:
- **Be technically sound**
- Assess the **relative contribution** of cognitive, behavior, physical, and developmental factors

Assessment tools and strategies must provide **relevant information** that directly assists in determining the student's educational needs.

3. District administers tests and other necessary procedures to produce the indicated data.

4. A team of "qualified professionals"** and the parents draw upon the evaluation data and determine whether:
   - Student has a disability as defined by the IDEA
   - Because of the disability needs special education

   A student may not be determined to have a disability if the determinant factor is either lack of instruction in reading or math or limited English proficiency.

5. District gives parents a copy of the evaluation report and documentation of eligibility determination.

* "Qualified professionals" are persons who possess the knowledge and skills to interpret evaluation data and make an informed determination as to whether a student has a disability as defined in the IDEA and to determine whether the student needs special education and related services. Who these persons are in any particular case depends upon the student's suspected disability.

If suspected disability is specific learning disability (SLD):

- IEP team must include the student's regular teacher or another regular classroom teacher qualified to teach students of the same age and at least one person qualified to conduct individual diagnostic tests of children
- At least one team member other than the regular teacher must observe student's academic performance in the classroom
- Team may diagnose SLD if student is not achieving commensurate with age and ability and assessment reveals a severe discrepancy between ability and achievement
- Team may not diagnose SLD if discrepancy results from sensory impairments, mental retardation, emotional disturbance, or "environmental, cultural, or economic disadvantage"
- Team must document its determination in a written report, and dissenting members must prepare a separate statement

The following "Do's and Don'ts" are derived from the law and from observation of practice in the real world.

Do's: Evaluation and Identification

1. **Do** notify the child's parents about the proposed evaluation and obtain their written consent before conducting an initial evaluation, administering any new test as part of a reevaluation, or other circumstances as required by state law or district policy. Remember that parents may withdraw their consent.

2. **Do** ask parents to participate in the evaluation and identification process and consider their input as evaluation data.

3. **Do** inform parents that they have a legal right to an independent educational evaluation at public expense if they disagree with the district's evaluation.

4. **Do** consider requesting a due process hearing or mediation if a child's need for special education is clear but parents refuse consent for evaluation or reevaluation.

5. **Do** use a variety of assessment materials and strategies that provide sufficient information to: (1) judge whether the child fits into one of the IDEA eligibility categories; (2) decide if the child, because of the disability, needs special education; and (3) assess the child's educational needs and determine the content of the child's IEP.

6. **Do** administer tests and other assessment materials in the child's native language or other appropriate mode of communication.

Don'ts: Evaluation and Identification

1. **Don't** single out a child for testing, interviewing, or overt observation without notice to parents. Beware of "prereferral intervention" programs which have the effect of delaying an eligible child's special education evaluation or IEP.

2. **Don't** equate evaluation with testing. Evaluation should also include observations, work samples, interviews, information provided by parents, cumulative files, etc. No one test comes close to being an adequate evaluation, legally or professionally.

3. **Don't** rely on any standardized battery of assessments, and most definitely don't select tests solely from those "tabled" for use in a formula or for any other purposes.

4. **Don't** rely exclusively on any formula or quantitative guideline to determine eligibility. The more elaborate the formula, the sillier it will appear to a judge. The law requires the exercise of professional judgment.

5. **Don't** ask a professional, such as a physician or psychiatrist, whether a child has a particular disability. Instead, provide the IDEA disability definition, and ask whether the child fits that definition.

6. **Don't** use evaluation methods that discriminate on the basis of race, culture, or native language. Evaluation that discriminates on the basis of sex is forbidden by other Federal laws (ESEA, Title IX), but the well-known fact that roughly twice as many boys as girls are in special education suggests that this prohibition is widely disregarded.

Individualized Education Program and Related Services (Program Planning)

Any child found eligible for IDEA services is entitled to an IEP. An IEP is a written document that describes a child's educational needs and details the special education and related services the district will provide to address those needs. The IDEA lays out mandatory procedures for IEP development. Among other things, the law prescribes the membership of the team that designs an IEP, and it outlines the required components of an IEP. It's possible that Congress succeeded in its intention of reducing some IDEA paperwork, but we regret to say that such a change has not occurred in the IEP process. To the contrary, IEP requirements have been greatly expanded, as have the responsibilities of the IEP team. The remaining chapters of this book explore these requirements in detail, but brief highlights follow here.

Do's: Program Planning

1. **Do** individualize the child's program.

2. **Do** base the IEP on the individual child's needs, not on the present availability of services in the district.

3. **Do** figure out what supports the child might need to participate in the general curriculum. If there is no need for modifications in the regular classroom, there is reason to question the child's eligibility.

4. **Do** consider the child's strengths and parents' concerns for enhancing their child's education.

5. **Do** specify all necessary special education, related services, supplementary aids and services, program modifications, and supports for school personnel.

6. **Do** include positive behavioral interventions and discipline strategies when there is reason to believe that behavior is an issue.

7. **Do** meticulously observe all procedural requirements for IEP development and content.

8. **Do** ensure meaningful parental participation.

Don'ts: Program Planning

1. **Don't** worry about "opening the floodgates." Providing certain services to one child does not set a precedent for other children. IEPs address the unique needs of individual children, so what one child needs has no implications for what the district must provide to others.

2. **Don't** clutter IEPs with detailed goals and objectives for all the content standards in the general curriculum. Instead, focus on the accommodations and adjustments an individual child needs for appropriate access to and participation in the general curriculum.

3. **Don't** include more than two or three objectives or benchmarks for each annual goal. Objectives and benchmarks should describe "how far, by when" the child should progress toward achievement of each annual goal.

4. **Don't** use lack of funds as an excuse for failure to provide a FAPE.

5. **Don't** ever provide services categorically! For example, don't say that only emotionally disturbed students may have behavioral components in their IEPs or that only students with learning disabilities may be allowed extra time on tests. All services must be based upon the individual child's needs without regard to disability category.

Placement

Placement lies at the center of an ideological storm in special education. Proponents of "full inclusion" insist that the proper learning environment for all children, with and without disabilities, is the regular classroom. The inclusionist movement has resulted in increased numbers of children with disabilities being placed full-time in regular classes. Many educators, adults with disabilities, and advocacy organizations are resisting this trend, arguing that full inclusion deprives many children of services they need to meet their unique educational needs.

While the storm rages, the law quietly remains unchanged. There is not now and has never been a requirement in the IDEA that all children with disabilities be "included" or "mainstreamed" in the regular classroom. In the 1997 Amendments, Congress removed any doubts about a possible change in Federal policy on this issue. The law continues to express a preference rather than a mandate for placement of children with disabilities in the regular classroom:

(5) Least Restrictive Environment —

(A) In General- To the maximum extent appropriate, children with disabilities, including children in public or private institutions or other care facilities, are educated with children who are not disabled, and special classes, separate schooling, or other removal of children with disabilities from the regular educational environment occurs only when the nature or severity of the disability of a child is such that education in regular classes with the use of supplementary aids and services cannot be achieved satisfactorily (20 USC §1412(a)(5)(A)).

"To the maximum extent appropriate" is the key phrase here. The IDEA recognizes that regular classroom placement might be inappropriate for some children. Least restrictive environment (LRE) is not a synonym for regular classroom. Technically, LRE refers to a set of procedures and requirements found in the IDEA regulations at 34 CFR §§300.550-554.

The U.S. Supreme Court has held that a program is appropriate if it was developed according to the procedures required by the law and if it is "reasonably calculated" to allow the child to benefit educationally. The Court offered the following guidance on the measure of appropriateness for students who are mainstreamed:

> The IEP, and therefore the personalized instruction, should be formulated in accordance with the requirements of the Act and, if the child is being educated in the regular classroom of the public education system, should be reasonably calculated to enable the child to achieve passing marks and advance from grade to grade … (*Hendrick Hudson Bd. of Ed. v. Rowley*, 458 U.S. 176 (1982)).

In practice, a district cannot change a student's placement unilaterally if the parents object to the change. If parents request a hearing to challenge a proposed change in placement, the child remains in the current placement until all administrative or judicial proceedings are completed. A hearing officer's finding that it would be dangerous for the child to remain in the present setting is the only exception to this "stay put" provision.

One of the most contentious issues related to placement involves student discipline. Suspension for more than ten days and expulsion constitute changes in placement. Schools that use exclusionary discipline for students with disabilities must follow a strict set of procedures (see Figure 3), and districts must continue to provide FAPE to students who have been excluded for more than ten days. Districts should seek legal advice and proceed with caution before suspending or expelling students with IEPs.

Figure 3

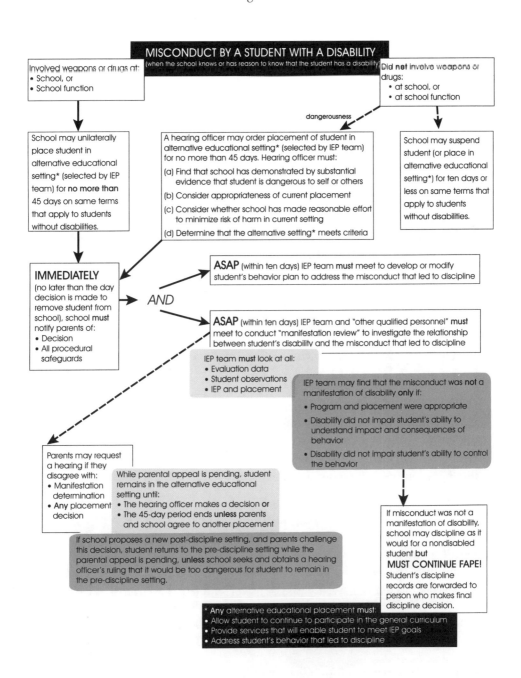

Do's: Placement

1. **Do** remember that program appropriateness is the primary IDEA mandate, and LRE is secondary. As a Federal district court judge has explained:

   > Nowhere in the Act is a handicapped child required to sink or swim in an ordinary classroom.... Congress certainly did not intend to place handicapped children in a least restrictive environment and thereby deny them an appropriate education (*Visco v. Sch. Dist. of Pittsburgh*, 684 F.Supp. 1310 (1988)).

2. **Do** make available a continuum of various alternative placements, including resource rooms, special classes, special schools, etc., so children with disabilities can learn in the environment that is appropriate for them, based upon their individual needs.

3. **Do** determine each child's placement at least annually and individually, basing the decision on the child's IEP.

4. **Do** ensure that each placement decision is made by a group of persons, including parents, who are knowledgeable about the child, the meaning of the evaluation data, and the placement options.

5. **Do** consider any potential harmful effects on the child or on the quality of services when selecting the LRE.

6. **Do** make sure each child is educated and otherwise participates with nondisabled children to the maximum extent appropriate.

7. **Do** place each child in the school he or she would attend if nondisabled unless the IEP requires some other arrangement.

Don'ts: Placement

1. **Don't** remove a child with a disability from the regular education environment unless the disability is such that education in regular classes cannot be achieved satisfactorily, even with the use of supplementary aids and services.

2. **Don't** substitute a policy of "full inclusion" for the continuum of various alternative placements required by the IDEA.

3. **Don't** exclude parents from placement decisions.

4. **Don't** forget to follow all the procedural requirements for all "changes of placement" including suspension of more than ten days, expulsion, graduation, and significant program changes.

5. **Don't** ever place a student on the basis of his or her disability category! Regardless of disability category, placement must be based upon the student's IEP.

Funding

Special education and related services can be expensive, and the IDEA clearly places the financial burden of educating students with disabilities on school districts. The "F" in FAPE means free to parents. There are no exceptions to the requirement that school districts make available a **free** appropriate public education to all children who have a disability and need special education.

Normally, cost may not be a consideration at all in selection of a child's program or placement. If evaluation reveals that a child with a disability needs a particular service, the district must provide that service even if it is costly. No court has ever allowed consideration of cost for common services, such as reading tutors or daily speech therapy.

In a few narrowly-defined circumstances, cost may be a factor. For example, a district may select the less expensive of two equally suitable facilities for a child who requires residential placement. One circuit court of appeals has ruled that a district should consider costs for a placement so expensive as to impact the budget and significantly reduce the resources available to the other children in the district (*Greer v. Rome City Sch. Dist.*, 950 F.2d 688 (11th Cir., 1991)).

Failure to provide FAPE can be very costly to a district. Parents who believe their child's IEP is not appropriate may unilaterally place their child in a private school that does provide an appropriate program. Under most circumstances, parents must first notify the district of their dissatisfaction with the offered program and of their intent to enroll the child in a private school at public expense. A district that receives such a notice should be very certain that its proposed program constitutes FAPE, or it may be ordered to reimburse parents for the cost of the private school. The U.S. Supreme Court has advised that:

> … public educational authorities who want to avoid reimbursing parents for the private education of a disabled child can do one of two things: give the child a free

appropriate public education in a public setting, or place the child in an appropriate private setting of the State's choice. This is IDEA's mandate, and school officials who conform to it need not worry about reimbursement claims (*Florence County Sch. Dist. Four v. Carter*, 510 US 7 (1993))

Do's: Funding

1. **Do** base the content of a child's IEP on his or her unique educational needs without considering the cost of meeting those needs at least sufficiently to constitute FAPE.

2. **Do** make available a continuum of various alternative placements. Cost is no excuse for failure to do so. Small districts may not be able to maintain every conceivable placement a child might need, in which case they may choose to join in regional service plans, contract with other districts or private facilities, etc.

3. **Do** remember that attempts to cut corners can backfire. If the district fails to provide an appropriate program, parents can unilaterally place their child in an expensive private facility that does offer an appropriate program, and the district may have to pay for it.

Don'ts: Funding

1. **Don't** compel parents to use private insurance to pay for any services a child needs in order to benefit from special education. If parents voluntarily use their insurance, the district must compensate them for any increases in premiums or reductions in benefits.

2. **Don't** use a related service provider's schedule as a limiting factor on the amount of service available to a child. Districts must determine the frequency and duration of services case-by-case, based upon the individual needs of each child.

3. **Don't** cite unavailability of personnel as a justification for failure to provide needed services. Districts should employ outside contractors if this is necessary to address a child's needs.

4. **Don't** arbitrarily take a hard line with parents who disagree with their child's IEP. This is a high stakes gamble that the district can lose if it fails to offer

FAPE and parents place their child in a private school that does offer an appropriate program.

Procedural Safeguards

Built into the IDEA is an elaborate system of procedural safeguards designed to ensure access to FAPE for children with disabilities (3 CFR §§300.500-517). Although a detailed discussion of procedural safeguards is beyond the scope of this book, a few points deserve mention here.

Parents have a right to participate in all meetings scheduled for the purpose of discussing their child's identification, evaluation, program, or placement. Districts should keep records that demonstrate a diligent effort to ensure parental participation. Parents need not be invited to informal or chance meetings or to staff meetings held for the purpose of preparing for a meeting with parents (34 CFR §300.501).

The IDEA requires parental consent before initial evaluation, initial placement in special education, and administration of any new test during a reevaluation. State law may include additional consent requirements. If parents refuse consent, a district may attempt mediation or may seek a hearing officer's order to proceed without consent if that appears to be in the best interests of the child. When considering actions that do not require consent, districts must still provide prior notice, and parents who disagree with the district's plans may file a complaint, initiate mediation, or request a hearing (34 CFR §300.505).

Procedural safeguards are effective only when parents know about and make use of them. School districts must provide parents with clear, detailed, and understandable explanations of their IDEA rights. This notice must explain all safeguards related to: (1) independent educational evaluation; (2) parental notice and consent; (3) access to records; (4) students attending private schools; (5) opportunities to present complaints; (6) dispute resolution processes, including mediation, hearings, and civil actions; (7) the child's placement during dispute resolution proceedings—the "stay put" provision; (8) procedures relating to suspension and expulsion; and (9) payment of attorneys' fees (34 CFR §300.504).

Do's: Procedural Safeguards

1. **Do** send parents prior written notice of proposed actions regarding their child. Parents are entitled to notice any time a district proposes or refuses to initiate or changes anything about the child's identification, evaluation, program, or placement. Notice must explain the district's proposed action, inform parents of their rights, and be provided in a form that parents can understand.

2. **Do** give parents a complete procedural safeguards notice when: (1) their child is referred for evaluation, (2) an IEP meeting is scheduled, (3) the child needs reevaluation, and/or (4) a parent requests a due process hearing. Make sure this notice is provided in parents' native language, and avoid the use of jargon.

3. **Do** make mediation available in order to resolve disputes between parents and schools in a nonadversarial fashion.

4. **Do** provide parents with a genuine opportunity to participate in all meetings relating to their child.

5. **Do** notify parents and student in advance if state law provides for the transfer of parental rights to the student when he or she reaches the age of majority as defined by state law.

Don'ts: Procedural Safeguards

1. **Don't** take any action regarding a child's identification, evaluation, program, or placement without sending written notice to parents in advance.

2. **Don't** put pressure on parents to use mediation, and don't use mediation to delay or deny parents' right to a due process hearing or to any other rights.

3. **Don't** restrict parents' access to their child's education records. Parents have a right to examine all their child's records, including student response forms for all tests.

Figure 4 illustrates the interrelationships among the five IDEA components just introduced. The three sequential components—evaluation, program, and placement—rest on a solid foundation of procedural safeguards, and public funding of all components ensures that all children with disabilities enjoy equal access to an appropriate education.

Figure 4

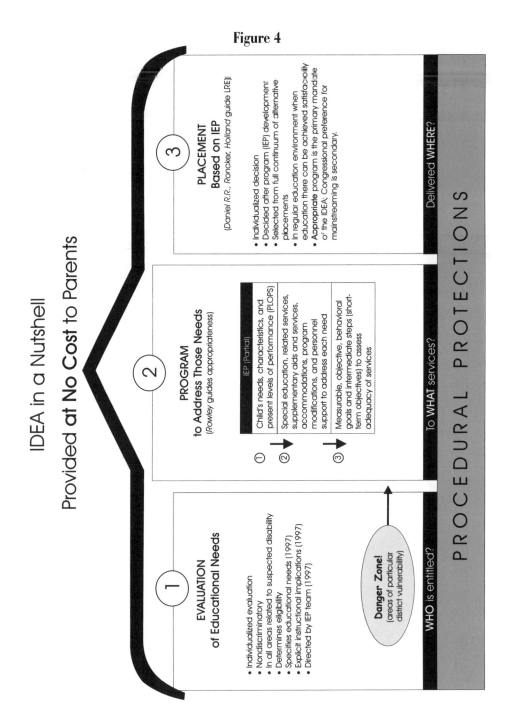

Summary

The "IDEA Commandments" (see Figure 5) were handed down in 1977 from "Mount Deecee" to public schools throughout the land. School districts will defy these commandments at their peril!

Figure 5

IDEA COMMANDMENTS

I. THOU SHALT BASE ALL ELIGIBILITY DECISIONS ON PROFESSIONAL JUDGMENT, NOT ON QUANTITATIVE FORMULAE.

II. THOU SHALT OPEN WIDE THE DOOR UNTO EVERY NEEDED SERVICE AND PLACEMENT FOR EACH ELIGIBLE CHILD.

III. REMEMBER THOU THAT CATEGORICAL DELIVERY OF SERVICES IS AN ABOMINATION.

IV. EACH IEP SHALL BE BASED SOLELY UPON THE CHILD'S NEEDS. HE OR SHE WHO LOOKS INSTEAD TO AVAILABILITY OF SERVICES SHALL KNOW THE INFERNO.

V. MAKETH EVERY IEP IN THE IMAGE OF ITS CHILD. AN IEP LIKE UNTO ANOTHER IS A GRAVEN IMAGE, DESPISED BY ALL WHO KNOW IDEA.

VI. PLACE NOT ALL CHILDREN IN THE SAME SETTING, BUT MAKE AVAILABLE THE ENTIRE CONTINUUM OF ALTERNATIVE PLACEMENTS.

VII. THOU SHALT NOT EXCLUDE PARENTS FROM DECISIONS THAT AFFECT THEIR CHILDREN.

VIII. THOU SHALT NOT BURDEN PARENTS WITH THE COST OF THEIR CHILDREN'S SPECIAL EDUCATION AND SERVICES.

The Legally Correct IEP

The most important thing to be said for legal, technical, and procedural correctness is that it goes a long way toward ensuring a meaningful, useful IEP. It isn't a guarantee, but it surely is a good start. On the other side of the coin, the big risk in failing to employ squeaky clean procedures is that the program which results could be declared inappropriate, even though in every other way it was fine. This finding of an inappropriate program, in turn, can obligate the school district to pay for parentally obtained private services, even a residential placement. So, developing IEPs is serious business. A great deal is at stake, most especially the education of children.

In one typical case, the administrative law judge ruled that the remedy for the district's procedural violations was to award reimbursement for all the costs of a private residential placement plus physical therapy three times per week and daily language and occupational therapies. The procedural violations included: (1) the amount of related services offered was based not on the student's individual needs but on the district's predetermined service schedule; (2) an IEP meeting was held without a district representative who had the power to allocate district resources; (3) the IEP goals were the same as the previous year; (4) the IEP failed to contain objective, measurable criteria, and evaluation procedures; and (5) the district failed to consider the need for extended school year (ESY) (GA. SEA, *Cobb Co. S.D.*, 26 IDELR 229 (1997)).

Parental expenses for tutoring and more were awarded in another leading case because of these too common procedural errors by the district: (1) an IEP was developed with no input from the private school the student was attending; (2) the IEP proposed placing the student in a preexisting, predetermined program; and (3) the district failed to consider the recommendations of the people most knowledgeable about the student. Together these violations showed the IEP was not reasonably calculated to allow educational benefit (*W.G. v. Target Range S.D.*, 960 F.2d. 1479 (9th Cir., 1992)). One district's change in placement was invalidated by a court because of the district's failure to have a district representative present at the IEP meeting (*Smith v. Henson*, 786 F.Supp. 43 (D.D.C., 1992)). In general, the courts have taken the position that minor procedural flaws will be overlooked provided the essence of the process was intact, the parents had an opportunity for meaningful participation, and the result was an otherwise appropriate program (see, e.g., *Doe v. Defendant I*, 898 F.2d 1186 (6th Cir., 1990)). Major procedural flaws, however, will likely be a denial of FAPE and can result in awards such as those described.

Among the most vital principles of IEP development, about which there will be little if any judicial forgiving or overlooking, are these:

- Parents must have a genuine opportunity for full participation in the IEP process.

- The services offered—special education, related services, supplementary aids and services, modifications, personnel support and accommodations—absolutely must be based on the child's needs, not on the availability of services. This principle is equally true of the placement decision which must be based on the IEP.

- The parents must be given full notice of all their procedural rights related to their child's services, as well as to all other aspects of his or her education.

This chapter will examine these and more principles related to **who** is on the IEP team, **how** the IEP team functions, **when** the IEP team meets, **where** the IEP team meets and must it do so, and finally, exactly **what** a proper IEP contains.

Much of the information in this chapter is found in two Department of Education Policy Interpretations, both called "Appendix C to Part 300—Notice of Interpretation." One is dated 1981, and the new one 1998. Not coincidentally portions of those documents appear as Appendix C in this book. They are a vital source of information for anyone who wishes to be knowledgeable about IEPs. Our premise is that the portions of the 1981 Appendix C that are not dealt with and/or are not in conflict with the 1998 Appendix C still offer good guidance and advice.

Who Is the IEP Team?

For all IEP meetings the following participants are required:

(1) The parents (or surrogate parent) of the child;

(2) At least one regular education teacher of the child (if the child is, or may be, participating in the regular education environment);

(3) At least one special education teacher, or if appropriate, at least one special education provider of the child;

(4) A representative of the local education agency (LEA) who —

   (i) Is qualified to provide, or supervise the provision of, specially designed instruction to meet the unique needs of children with disabilities;

   (ii) Is knowledgeable about the general curriculum; and

   (iii) Is knowledgeable about the availability of resources of the LEA;

(5) An individual who can interpret the instructional implications of evaluation results, who may be a member of the team described above;

(6) At the discretion of the parent or the school, other individuals who have knowledge or special expertise regarding the child, including related service personnel as appropriate; and

(7) The student, if age 14 or older, must be invited. Younger students may attend if appropriate (34 CFR 300.344).

In addition, if transition needs or services (i.e., those for post-school life) are being considered a representative must be invited from any agency likely to be funding or providing such services. The student must also be invited and, if he or she does not attend, his or her interests and preferences must nonetheless be considered in the transition plan. If an invited agency representative does not attend the school must take other steps to obtain the agency's participation. The general rule is that anyone who has special knowledge of or expertise about the child may attend an IEP meeting if invited. However, that does not include a representative of a teacher organization who would be there on behalf of a teacher rather than the child (1981 Appendix C, Question 20).

The formal procedural safeguards notice requirements of 34 CFR 300.504 do not apply to IEP meetings themselves. In other words parents need not be given a formal notice of an IEP meeting, but rather they are invited to participate in a meeting scheduled for a certain time and place (Letter to O'Connor, 26 IDELR 320 (OSEP, 1996)). However, a copy of all procedural safeguards must be given upon each invitation to an IEP meeting (34 CFR 300.504(a)). The parents must also be informed, at least by title or role, of who will be attending for the district. The parents need not, however, tell the district who, if anyone, they will invite to the IEP meeting.

The Parent

"Parent" is used more broadly in the IDEA than some realize. The term includes a parent, guardian, or surrogate parent appointed according to 34 CFR 300.515. If a state elects to do so it may also recognize willing foster parents who have no conflict of interest if they have an ongoing, long-term parental relationship and the natural parents no longer have the legal authority to make educational decisions for the child (34 CFR 300.19 and note).

Any errors that are made in deciding who is a parent or which parent should participate in the IEP process should be made on the side of inclusion, rather than exclusion, since both the district and the parent may bring any knowledgeable person they wish to an IEP meeting. The only exception is when the district has written, official documentation that a person is not to function in the parental role and a person who is so authorized wishes to exclude him or her.

Special Education and Regular Education Teachers

The importance of teachers being at the IEP meeting is indisputable. A decision reached in a New York IEP meeting prior to the teacher's arrival was invalid (N.Y. SEA, *Bd. of Ed. of City of N.Y.*, 24 IDELR 199 (1996)). More dramatically, the absence of teachers who knew the student well was a denial of FAPE in several cases (e.g., *W.G. v. Target Range, supra* and *Brimmer v. Traverse City P.S.*, 872 F.Supp. 447 (W.D. Mich., 1994)). The role of teachers in the IEP process is critical. Beginning with all IEPs in effect on July 1, 1998, the IDEA requires that a regular education teacher be present, in addition to the special education teacher, if the student is or may be participating in regular education. A note to 34 CFR 300.344 discusses the regular and special education teachers:

> The regular education teacher participating in a child's IEP meeting should be the teacher who is, or may be, responsible for implementing the IEP, so that the teacher can participate in discussions about how best to teach the child.

> If the child has more than one teacher, the LEA may designate which teacher or teachers will participate. In a situation in which all of the child's teachers do not participate in the IEP meeting, the LEA is encouraged to seek input from teachers who will not be attending, and should ensure that any teacher not attending the meeting is informed about the results of the meeting (including receiving a copy of the IEP). In the case of a child whose behavior impedes the learning of the child or others, the LEA is encouraged to have a person knowledgeable about positive behavior strategies at the IEP meeting.

> Similarly, the special education teacher should be the person who is or will be responsible for implementing the student's IEP.

Perhaps this dual "responsibility for implementing the IEP" issue will be resolved or changed in the final IDEA regulations. If not, districts must address it very carefully and specifically so that someone is squarely in charge of IEP implementation.

The 1998 admonition that any of the student's teachers who are not at the IEP meeting should receive copies of the IEP is a welcome change in the law that will be discussed later. It is the unusual to rare situation in which a properly eligible student does not need, at a minimum, some accommodations or modifications in the regular class activities which must be included in the IEP and known to all the student's teachers.

The District (Agency) Representative

The Department of Education has answered the frequently asked question: "Who can serve as the 'representative of the public agency' at an IEP meeting?"

> The IEP team must include a representative of the local educational agency who: (a) is qualified to provide, or supervise the provision of, specially designed instruction to meet the unique needs of children with disabilities; (b) is knowledgeable about the general curriculum; (c) is knowledgeable about the availability of resources of the local educational agency (Sec. 300.344(a)(4)). Each State or local agency may determine which specific staff member will serve as the agency representative in a particular IEP meeting, so long as the individual meets these requirements. It is, however, important that the agency representative have the authority

to commit agency resources and be able to ensure that whatever services are set out in the IEP will actually be provided.

Note: IEP meetings for continuing placements may in some instances be more routine than those for initial placements, and, thus, may not require the participation of a key administrator (1998 Appendix C, Question 22).

The district representative must actually participate in the IEP meeting. An agency ruling has prohibited the practice of the representative, often the building administrator, putting in only a perfunctory, brief appearance (*Davila*, 18 IDELR 1036 (OSERS, 1992)). Notice that according to Appendix C, it is important that the representative have the authority to commit agency resources. The parent should always ascertain that there is a district person present who has that allocation power and know who that person is. The common sense rule is to never accept "No" from someone who doesn't have the power to say "Yes." Note also that the representative must be able to ensure the services set out in the IEP will be provided and are not subject to veto from above. These requirements reveal that all of the power to determine what services are needed, and therefore will be provided, rests with the IEP team and with no one else. This must be understood by all parties. Not even the school board can change any part of the IEP (*Schrag*, 18 IDELR 627 (OSEP, 1991)).

The "Instructional Implications of Evaluation" Person

A new requirement for all IEP team meetings after July 1, 1998 is the presence of a person knowledgeable about the instructional implications of the evaluation results. The long-term results of this requirement may range from none at all to marked improvement in the quality of IEPs. If a district responds simply by claiming that the teachers and/or the district representative already required to be there have that expertise, the only possible positive effect would be drawing the team's attention to the necessity for determining and exploring the instructional implications in the evaluation data. In the past, the use of evaluation data has often been limited to determining eligibility and the IEP team has begun its deliberations either by setting goals for the student or by deciding on services or even placement—all inappropriate starting places. The only appropriate starting point is with the unique needs of the child as determined by the evaluation.

The new twin requirements for an "instructional implications" person and for the specification of educational needs have the strong possibility, if taken seriously and acted upon, of greatly improving the quality of IEPs. If the IEP process begins with specification of the child's needs a major step will have been taken toward a better IEP.

"Others"

The ideal IEP team is small, is knowledgeable about the district, the law, and the child, and is focused on the needs of the child. However, in some disputed or complex situations the meeting can become very large. Obviously when 15 or 20 people are present the nature of the meeting has been changed. A common practice is for related service personnel such as speech therapists or physical therapists to be present. Note that the law allows but does not require that related service personnel be present (*Butler*, EHLR 213:118 (OSERS, 1988); 34 CFR 300.344 (a)(6)). It is perhaps more appropriate to encourage their written participation. For example, a recommended service schedule (i.e., nature, frequency, location, and amount of service) could be sent by the related service provider to the IEP team participants, including the parents, prior to the meeting. Only if there was a particular issue a related service provider wanted to address would he or she need to attend (1998 Appendix C, Question 27).

Prevailing parents' attorneys will no longer be paid fees for attending IEP meetings, except when the meeting has been ordered by a hearing officer or judge, so fewer parents' attorneys might be expected to attend IEP meetings in the future.

The Student

Until the student reaches age 14, the parents decide whether he or she is to be part of the IEP team. The district should so inform all parents and provide guidance or information if appropriate. It is common that younger students attend a portion of the meeting but not all. This practice allows for genuine participation and "ownership" by the student but also accommodates the frequent need to discuss matters that might be inappropriate were the student present for the entire time. However beginning at age 14, the student is an integral part of the IEP team and should attend the entire meeting.

Certain limitations regarding IEP and FAPE entitlements apply to persons over age 18 who are incarcerated (see 34 CFR 300.311 for details).

How Does the IEP Team Function?

The primary job of the IEP team is to plan a program of special education and related services (including needed modifications and accommodations in the regular classroom) which is reasonably calculated to enable the child to receive educational benefit. Special education is defined as "... specially designed instruction ... to meet the unique needs of a child" (34 CFR 300.24(a)(1)). "Specially designed instruction" means "... adapting content, methodology, or delivery of instruction" to meet the unique needs of the child and ensure access to the general curriculum (34 CFR 300.24(b)(3)). Thus, it is apparent the IEP team must focus on the individual child's unique needs and ways to meet those needs.

New attention is directed to specification of unique needs in the 1997 Amendments. Now evaluations must lead directly to the specification of educational needs. Furthermore, every IEP meeting must be attended by someone able to interpret the instructional implications of evaluation, the most recent of which must be considered by the team. The IEP itself must address the student's needs relative to accessing the general curriculum and all other needs arising from the disability.

IEP team participants should come to the meeting prepared to explicitly enumerate the student's needs. The following examples are all student needs as expressed by Federal judges: a need for reteaching and repetition, small classes, flexible programming, computer access and training, a highly structured environment, frequent teacher feedback, individualized attention, consistent behavior management, a need to be with other students with similar needs, and a need for full-time learning support and extended school year (e.g., *Capistrano Unified S.D. v. Wartenberg*, 59 F.3d 884 (9th Cir., 1995); *Evans v. Bd. of Rhinebeck Central S.D.*, 930 F.Supp. 83 (S.D.N.Y., 1996)).

A model first IEP letter of invitation (see Figure 18 in Chapter Four) would inform the parents of the meeting's focus on their child's unique needs or characteristics, the planning of services needed to allow him or her to receive benefit, and the parents' equal-to-district role in determining these. Examples of helpful parental input and descriptions of some of the needs of children similar to their child could be included. Above all, the parents should be asked to come to the meeting prepared to share ways in which they would like the district to individualize their child's educational program. The law now requires that the IEP team must consider the strengths of the child and the concerns of the parents for enhancing their child's education (34 CFR 300.346(a)). Parents need to know this.

The parents and district personnel may and should come to the meeting prepared with suggestions to put on the table for discussion (*Louisiana Dept. of Ed.*, EHLR 213:230 (OSEP, 1989)). The actual IEP is then developed with full, equal parental participation. Too often districts fail to establish any understanding by or expectations for the parents other than that the IEP meeting is a teacher-parent "conference" in which the school tells the parents how things are going to be.

In many instances the lines between the IEP process itself and the evaluation or identification process, and between the IEP process and the placement decision, are substantially blurred with no detrimental effects. Evaluation results must certainly be discussed at the IEP meeting and the importance of the IEP team member who can interpret the instructional implications of evaluation cannot be overstated. Let us all hope there is enough of that invaluable expertise to stretch to the more than five million IEP meetings held each year. Under the 1997 Amendments, evaluation reports must now contribute potentially useful information about the child's needs and how to meet them, whereas in the past the only relevance of some evaluations to program planning was that they established the child's entitlement to an IEP.

The parents now have the right to participate in all meetings about their child, whether the meeting deals with evaluation, identification, program, or placement (34 CFR 300.501 (a)(2)), so it will be easier than ever to discuss any and all of these matters. As a general rule that should not pose major risks. However, when placement is on the agenda, the IEP team must take extra care to ensure that the placement decision is based on the already completed IEP (see Figures 1 and 4 in Chapter One) and that persons knowledgeable about the child, the placement options, and the evaluation data make the decision (34 CFR 300.552 (a)(1) and note 1). Moreover, if a placement decision is to be made at the meeting, the school must use additional means to obtain parental participation, including individual or conference calls, or video conferencing (34 CFR 300.501 (c)(3)).

Just as extra care is required in dealing with placement in the IEP meeting, so the sequence of addressing evaluation and the IEP is also critical in that the needs of the child, as determined by the evaluation, must be the starting point for meaningful IEP development. In other words, the order of business in an all-purpose IEP meeting must be to first address the child's eligibility and unique needs as determined by the evaluation, then the IEP itself, and finally, placement. Each builds on its predecessor.

Another reason for conceptually and sequentially separating evaluation, the IEP, and placement is that many of the serious disputes that arise under the IDEA are about placement. This has been true in the past and is becoming ever more so. Often the sequence of procedural "technicalities," such as the order of these discussions, is vital in the legal resolution of these disputes. Specifically, the district is required to send prior written notice of a proposed placement or change in placement (with reasons, options considered, and more, as required by 34 CFR 300.503) and wait a reasonable time, usually understood as ten days. If the parents request a hearing to dispute the proposed placement, the "stay put" provision of the IDEA (34 CFR 300.514) is triggered and the child stays in the present placement until the hearing and some, if not all, appeal procedures are completed, unless the parents and district agree otherwise. If the parents do not request a hearing, the new placement may be made after the ten days and is then considered the present placement. The significance of this is that if the parents now request a hearing the child must stay put in the new placement.

The district must allow the parents to participate in the placement decision in the same full way they do in IEP development, and must pay special attention to procedural correctness. IEP procedural violations may invalidate a proposed change in placement (*Smith v. Henson*, 18 IDELR 897 (D.D.C., 1992)) and the failure to base a proposed change in placement on a revised IEP can be denial of FAPE entitling the student to remain in a private placement at public expense (*Spielberg v. Henrico Co.*, 853 F.2d 256 (4th Cir., 1988)).

What happens if a dispute arises during the IEP meeting? The Department of Education has addressed this issue at some length:

> The IEP meeting serves as a communication vehicle between parents and school personnel, and enables them, as equal participants, to make joint, informed decisions regarding the child's needs and appropriate goals, the extent to which the child will be involved in the general curriculum and participate in the regular education environment and State and district-wide assessments, and the services needed to support that involvement and participation and to achieve agreed-upon goals. Parents are to be equal partners with school personnel in making these decisions, and the IEP team must consider parents' concerns and information that they

provide regarding their child in developing and reviewing IEPs (Secs. 300.343(c)(iii) and 300.346 (a)(1) and (b)).

The IEP team should work toward consensus, but the public agency has ultimate responsibility to ensure that the IEP includes the services that the child needs in order to receive FAPE. **If it is not possible to reach consensus** [authors' emphasis] in an IEP meeting, the public agency must provide the parents with prior written notice of the agency's proposals or refusals, or both, regarding the child's educational program and placement, and the parents have the right to seek resolution of any disagreements through mediation or other informal means, or by initiating an impartial due process hearing. Every effort should be made to resolve differences between parents and school staff through voluntary mediation or some other informal step, without resort to a due process hearing. However, mediation or other informal procedures may not be used to deny or delay a parent's right to a due process hearing (1998 Appendix C, Question 9).

The IDEA does not require that parents sign IEPs, but it is common practice for all team members to sign and there is probably no reason not to do so. Technically, the signatures do little more than verify participation, as the district is obligated to provide the services on the IEP, regardless of who, if anyone, signs for the district. And if the parents' signatures are construed as written consent, no harm results because the parents can withdraw that consent at any time (34 CFR 300.500(b)(1)(iii)). For monitoring and compliance reasons, the district must document who participated in the meeting and so it is reasonable to use signatures for that purpose.

Another procedural concern is whether an IEP meeting may be either audio or videotape recorded. Neither the IDEA nor any other Federal statute speaks to this question. As a result, a variety of positions have been taken on this question, both by the courts and by the Office of Special Education Programs (OSEP). The current OSEP position is that:

> … Therefore, an SEA or public agency has the option to require, prohibit, limit, or otherwise regulate the use of recording devices at IEP meetings. If a public agency has a policy prohibiting the use of these devices at IEP meetings, that policy must provide for exceptions if they are necessary to ensure that the parent understands the IEP or the IEP process or to implement other parental rights guaranteed under Part B. Any recording of an IEP meeting that is maintained by the public agency is an "education record," within the meaning of the Family Educational Rights and Privacy Act ("FERPA"; 20 U.S.C. 1232g), and would, therefore, be subject to the confidentiality requirements of the regulations under both FERPA (34 CFR Part 99) and Part B (Secs. 300.560-300.575). Parents wishing to use audio or video re-

cording devices at IEP meetings should consult State or local policies for further guidance (1998 Appendix C, Question 21).

As before, it is clear the school should allow audio or videotaping if the parents have a particular need such as a language difference or a learning disability (see, e.g., *V.W. v. Favolise*, 16 EHLR 1070 (D. Conn., 1990)).

In summary, the answer to how the IEP team functions is that it is a full, equal parent-district partnership which specifies the child's unique needs and the special services necessary to enable the child to receive educational benefit.

When Does the IEP Team Meet?

The IEP team meets: (1) in time to complete the first IEP within 30 days of the determination the child is IDEA eligible, and usually within 60 days of the parental consent to the initial evaluation (34 CFR 300.343, note); (2) at least annually thereafter, at any time during the year, to review the IEP; (3) whenever there is a significant change in the program; and (4) in response to any lack of expected progress toward the annual goals, any reevaluation, new information about the child provided by the parents, or the child's anticipated needs or other pertinent matters (34 CFR 300.343(c)).

The IEP team, including the parents, must also meet for several purposes in addition to developing, reviewing, and revising the IEP. These include: (1) reviewing existing evaluation data and identifying what if any new data are needed (34 CFR 300.533(a)); (2) developing and reviewing functional assessment and behavioral intervention plans; (3) determining whether the student's disability caused misconduct which has occurred; and (4) selecting alternative placements to which school authorities may order a student.

Relatively few issues arise around when the IEP team meets. One occasional concern is with the meaning of a "mutually agreed on time" as required by 34 CFR 300.345 (a)(2). District policies vary greatly. Saturday and evening IEP meetings are unheard of in some districts and common in others. At a minimum, parents of children with disabilities must be given the same consideration and flexibility in scheduling, if any, as are parents of children without disabilities.

An important determination must be made when a child with a disability moves into a new district. If the child's old IEP is not available, is believed by either the parent or new district to be inappropriate, or if the new district is incapable of implementing it as written, an IEP meeting must be held immediately.

The most difficult issues related to when to hold IEP meetings have to do with changes in program or placement. The first portion of the difficulty is that a change in placement must be preceded by a reevaluation (required by §504 of the Rehabilitation Act of 1973, 34 CFR 104.36) and then by changes in the IEP (see, e.g., *Spielberg v. Henrico Co. Pub. Sch.*, 853 F.2d 256 (4th Cir., 1988)).

The next problem is knowing what is meant by the term "change in placement." First, it does **not** mean a change in locale or building or even level of building. For example, moving a special class across town or going from elementary to middle school is not necessarily a change in placement. However, a significant change in program is a change in placement, although a change in schedule is not, unless the ramifications involve more than just schedule. Expulsion, long-term (more than ten days) suspension, and graduation are changes in placement. Each must therefore be preceded by an evaluation and an IEP meeting. However, as illustrated by the next section of this chapter, an IEP meeting may not have to be an actual meeting, just as a change in placement may not be an actual change in placement.

Where Does the IEP Team Meet (or Does It)?

Customarily, IEP meetings are held in the building where the child attends school. This is certainly a reasonable and sensible practice and no change is recommended as long as all participants feel it is working and they leave each meeting with the feeling that it was worthwhile. And in any case it seems very important that the child's first IEP meeting and the first IEP meeting in any new district should be a face-to-face, sit down arrangement if at all possible. Similarly, if there are serious questions or issues about an IEP, the meeting should be of a face-to-face, sit down variety.

Having said that, there may be a substantial number of IEP meetings that can be legally managed in a much simpler fashion. The emphasis of the law is on **parental participation**, not on any particular meeting format. In that spirit OSEP said several years ago that on a case-by-case basis, with all required participants agreeing, alternative methods of IEP conferencing are allowed (*Soffer*, EHLR 213:187 (OSEP, 1988)). At a minimum this would seem to include computer conferencing, telephone conference calls, and facsimile (FAX) exchanges. Possible advantages of such alternative methods could include better preparation by all parties and the obvious reduction in hassle and time required.

Individualized decision making and true agreement by all required participants underlie the proper use of an alternative meeting method. Such methods are recommended only when all the parties concerned agree that there is no harm or significant loss to the child's program.

In Chapter Four, when we mention the round oak table where the IEP is developed, we will all understand that this is but a symbol of open, clear, and positive communication.

What Must the IEP Contain?

The Federal requirements for the content of the IEP are straightforward. The individualized education program for each eligible child must include:

(1) A statement of the child's present levels of educational performance, including

    i.   How the child's disability affects the child's involvement and progress in the general curriculum; or

    ii. For preschool children, as appropriate, how the disability affects the child's participation in appropriate activities;

(2) A statement of measurable annual goals, including benchmarks or short-term objectives, related to

    i.   Meeting the child's needs that result from the child's disability to enable the child to be involved in and progress in the general curriculum; and

    ii. Meeting each of the child's other educational needs that result from the child's disability;

(3) A statement of the special education and related services and supplementary aids and services to be provided to the child, or on behalf of the child, and a statement of the program modifications or supports for school personnel that will be provided for the child

    i.   To advance appropriately toward attaining the annual goals;

ii. To be involved and progress in the general curriculum and to participate in extracurricular and other nonacademic activities; and

iii. To be educated and participate with other children with disabilities and non-disabled children

(4) An explanation of the extent, if any, to which the child will not participate with nondisabled children in the regular class and in the activities described in paragraph (3)

(5) i. A statement of any individual modifications in the administration of State or district-wide assessments of student achievement that are needed in order for the child to participate in the assessment; and

ii. If the IEP team determines that the child will not participate in a particular State or district-wide assessment of student achievement (or part of an assessment), a statement of

(A) Why that assessment is not appropriate for the child; and

(B) How the child will be assessed;

(6) The projected date for the beginning of the services and modifications described in paragraph (3) and the anticipated frequency, location, and duration of those services and modifications; and

(7) A statement of

i. How the child's progress toward the annual goals described in paragraph (2) will be measured; and

ii. How the child's parents will be regularly informed (through such means as periodic report cards), at least as often as parents are informed of their non-disabled children's progress, of

(A) Their child's progress toward the annual goals; and

(B) The extent to which that progress is sufficient to enable the child to achieve the goals by the end of the year.

(8) Transition services [Transition "services" if the child is 16 or older or transition service "needs" if the child is 14 or older] (34 CFR 300.347). [This component is presented more fully later in this chapter.]

In addition the IEP team must always consider the strengths of the child and the parents' concerns for enhancing their child's education (34 CFR 300.346(a)(1)). Documentation of this consideration on the IEP is strongly urged and will probably be required by states and districts.

Furthermore, under certain circumstances additional special factors must be considered and documented:

(1) In the case of a child whose behavior impedes his or her learning or that of others, consider, if appropriate, strategies, including positive behavioral interventions, strategies, and supports to address that behavior;

(2) In the case of a child with limited English proficiency, consider the language needs of the child as these needs relate to the child's IEP;

(3) In the case of a child who is blind or visually impaired, provide for instruction in Braille and the use of Braille unless the IEP team determines, after an evaluation of the child's reading and writing skills, needs, and appropriate reading and writing media (including an evaluation of the child's future needs for instruction in Braille or the use of Braille), that instruction in Braille or the use of Braille is not appropriate for the child;

(4) Consider the communication needs of the child, and in the case of a child who is deaf or hard of hearing, consider the child's language and communication needs, opportunities for direct communications with peers and professional personnel in the child's language and communication mode, academic level, and full range of needs, including opportunities for direct instruction in the child's language and communication mode; and

(5) Consider whether the child requires assistive technology devices and services.

If during any of these deliberations the IEP team determines the child needs a particular device or service (including an intervention, accommodation, or other program modification) in order to receive FAPE, a statement to that effect must be included in the IEP (34 CFR 300.346(a)(b)(c)).

Each of the legally required IEP components (see Figure 6) will be examined separately and, for the moment, without regard to the order in which they are discussed during the IEP development process.

Figure 6

IEP COMPONENTS

FOR ALL STUDENTS:

I. PRESENT LEVELS OF PERFORMANCE

II. MEASURABLE GOALS AND OBJECTIVES

III. ASSESSMENT STATUS

IV. NONPARTICIPATION WITH NONDISABLED STUDENTS

V. ALL NEEDED SERVICES FULLY DESCRIBED (AMOUNT, FREQUENCY, ETC.)

VI. PROGRESS REPORTING

FOR SOME STUDENTS:

VII. TRANSITION—INCLUDING TRANSFER OF PARENTAL RIGHTS TO STUDENTS

VIII. BEHAVIOR PLAN

IX. ESL NEEDS

X. BRAILLE

XI. COMMUNICATION NEEDS

XII. ASSISTIVE TECHNOLOGY

Present Levels of Performance (PLOPs)

The Department of Education's guidance is very explicit about the child's performance (PLOPs) and what must be stated about them on the IEP:

The statement of present levels of educational performance will be different for each handicapped child. Thus, determinations about the content of the statement for an individual child are matters that are left to the discretion of participants in the IEP meetings. However, the following are some points which should be taken into account in writing this part of the IEP.

The statement should accurately describe the effect of the child's handicap on the child's performance in any area of education that is affected, including: (1) academic areas (reading, math, communication, etc.), and (2) nonacademic areas (daily life activities, mobility, etc.). (Note: Labels such as "mentally retarded" or "deaf" may not be used as a substitute for the description of present levels of educational performance.)

The statement should be written in objective measurable terms, to the extent possible. Data from the child's evaluation would be a good source of such information. Test scores that are pertinent to the child's diagnosis might be included, where appropriate. However, the scores should be: (1) self-explanatory (i.e., they can be interpreted by all participants without the use of test manuals or other aids), or (2) an explanation should be included. Whatever test results are used should reflect the impact of the handicap on the child's performance. Thus, raw scores would not usually be sufficient.

There should be a direct relationship between the present levels of educational performance and the other components of the IEP. Thus, if the statement describes a problem with the child's reading skill, this problem should be addressed under both: (1) goals and objectives, and (2) specific special education and related services to be provided to the child (1981 Appendix C, Question 36).

The new 1998 Appendix C provides no further guidance beyond the basic directive that the statement of present levels of performance must include: (1) how the disability affects the student's involvement and progress in the general curriculum, and (2) for preschool children, how the disability affects participation in age-relevant developmental abilities or milestones that typically developing children of the same chronological age would perform or achieve (1998 Appendix C, Question 1).

A problem sometimes encountered with present levels of performance is that some teachers think they must copy reams of test data from other sources onto the IEP form. This is probably not necessary. If required it is because of state or district policy, not Federal rules. Documents such as evaluation reports or test protocols may be incorporated into the IEP, and could simply be attached. The risk in this is that the data might not be intelligible standing alone and that would be unacceptable.

The PLOPs must be written **only** in the areas of the child's unique needs which will be addressed by the special services. In effect, the PLOP becomes: (1) an objective descriptor of the unique need, and (2) the starting point for specifying services to address the need and to develop goals and objectives to evaluate the results of the services. Suppose, for example, a child needs better anger management skills. That is the unique need to which a specific service must be addressed. The PLOP might be that the child has ten to 15 inappropriate anger outbursts per week. Or suppose a child needs to learn accurate decoding skills to replace his or her present excessive guessing at unknown words. His or her PLOP might be that the child reads second grade material at 20-30 words per minute with five to eight errors and seldom, if ever, self-corrects. The PLOP is, in essence, a mandated, objective way of presenting a child's needs which the remainder of the IEP must then address. The PLOP also provides the beginning point against which progress must be assessed, so it must be measurably stated.

Measurable Annual Goals and Benchmarks or Short-Term Objectives

According to the 1998 Appendix C, the:

> … measurable annual goals, including benchmarks or short-term objectives, are instrumental to the strategic planning process used to develop and implement the IEP for each child with a disability. Once the IEP team has developed measurable annual goals for each child, the team can: (1) develop strategies that will be most effective in realizing those goals, and (2) develop measurable, intermediate steps (short-term objectives) or major milestones (benchmarks) that will enable families, students, and educators to monitor **progress** during the year, and, if appropriate, to revise the IEP consistent with the child's instructional needs (Question 1).

Thus the purposes of annual goals and benchmarks or objectives are to assess the appropriateness of the special services and to monitor the child's progress. They need be written only for the special services necessary to meet the child's needs arising from the disability, not for the childs' total program, unless all areas are so affected (1998 Appendix C, Question 4).

In practice the goals and objectives are often the first items addressed in the IEP meeting, or perhaps second after a discussion of evaluation test results and present levels of performance. The next chapter will describe a different procedure. Since the purpose of a goal is to assess the effectiveness of services, it would seem it should be written with the specific service already in mind. The danger in writing goals based solely on the child's level of performance is that they then are too easily limited to the areas of specific deficiency identified by one procedure or test.

There are IEPs in which the entire contents are nothing but a reflection of the Woodcock-Johnson (W-J) test, no more, no less. On one such IEP one goal was written in each of the sub-test areas in which the student was weak. The PLOP was the W-J score, the service was a check mark by "special education," and the goal was four months' progress as measured on the W-J. The PLOPs and the annual goals must indeed be directly related (see 1981 Appendix C, Question 38). However, the service to be assessed may be a better connector between the two than is a standardized test.

Every goal must have two or three benchmarks or objectives which are measurable, intermediate steps between the PLOP and the goal. The objectives are to be progress markers. They should state "how far (toward the goal), by when." The IDEA regulations specifically require that an IEP show how progress will be measured and that the parents be told if progress toward the goal is sufficient to allow the child to reach the goal by the end of the year (34 CFR 300.347 (a)(7)).

A common source of substantial difficulty and undue effort in writing IEPs is confusion about whether goals and objectives need to be written for the related services to be provided. Most people have assumed related services must have goals and objectives. However, this is incorrect.

Notice that the related service provider need not attend the IEP meeting and that his or her written input would address only the nature, frequency, location, and amount of services. No mention is made of goals and objectives.

If one assumes that a related service is being provided, as it should be, because it is necessary to enable the student to benefit from special education, then it follows logically that a goal which evaluates the effectiveness of the special education also evaluates the supporting related service. This is precisely the position now taken by OSEP:

> …[W]hile there is no Part B requirements that an IEP include **separate** annual goals or short-term instructional objectives for related services, the goals and objectives in the IEP must address all of the student's identified needs that the IEP team has determined warrant the provision of special education, related services, or sup-

plementary aids and services, and must enable the team to determine the effectiveness of each of those services.

For example, if the IEP team has determined that a student needs speech and language therapy services as a component of free appropriate public education (FAPE), the IEP must include goals and objectives that address the student's need to develop and/or improve communication-related skills. It would not be necessary, however, to label the goals and objectives as "speech therapy" goals and objectives. Therefore, if the IEP includes goals and objectives which appropriately address the student's need to develop communication-related skills, no additional or separate "therapy" goals and objectives would be required .... If a related service such as air conditioning is necessary to enable the student to attend school, but that service is not intended to increase the student's skills, no goals or objectives are necessary. Similarly, if transportation is being provided solely to enable the student to reach school, no goals or objectives are needed. If, however, instruction will be provided to the student to enable the student to increase the student's independence or improve the student's behavior or socialization during travel to school, then goals and objectives must be included to address the need to increase independence or improve behavior or socialization (*Letter to Hayden*, 22 IDELR 501 (OSEP, 1994)).

An important note to the new regulations explains that:

The new emphasis on participation in the general education curriculum is not intended by the Committee to result in major expansions in the size of the IEP or dozens of pages of detailed goals and benchmarks or objectives in every curricular content standard skill. The new focus is intended to produce attention to the accommodations and adjustments necessary for disabled children to access the general education curriculum and the special services which may be necessary for the appropriate participation in particular areas of the curriculum due to the nature of the disability (34 CFR 300.347, Note 3).

Special Education and Other Special Services

The IEP must include a statement (not a check mark or two) of the **special education, related services, supplementary aids and services, program modifications, and supports for school personnel** that are needed by or on behalf of the child to: (1) progress toward the annual goals, (2) be involved in and progress in the general curriculum and participate in extracurricular and other nonacademic activities, and (3) be educated and participate with children with and without disabilities (34 CFR 300.347(a)(3)).

The IEP must include all of the special education and other services needed by the child, whether or not they are available in the district. The IEP team's agreement that a service is needed gives rise to a commitment and a duty on the part of the district to provide the service, directly or indirectly:

> The public agency must ensure that all services set forth in the child's IEP are provided, consistent with the child's needs as identified in the IEP. It may provide each of those services directly, through its own staff resources; indirectly, by contracting with another public or private agency; or through other arrangements. In providing the services, the agency may use whatever State, local, Federal, and private sources of support are available for those purposes (see Sec. 300.301(a)), but the services must be at no cost to the parents, and the public agency remains responsible for ensuring that the IEP services are provided in a manner that appropriately meets the student's needs as specified in the IEP. The SEA and responsible public agency may not allow the failure of another agency to provide services described in the child's IEP to deny or delay the provision of FAPE to a child (1998 Appendix C, Question 28).

Each state must ensure that qualified (i.e., certified, licensed, registered, etc.) personnel provide these special education and related services under the IDEA. Paraprofessionals do not have to meet state qualification standards "… if they are not directly responsible for the provision of special education and related services to students with disabilities," and they provide these services "… only under the supervision" of qualified special education or related service personnel (*Wilson*, 18 IDELR 276 (OSEP, 1991)). Under the IDEA, only students who need special education are eligible for services; therefore all IDEA students need special education provided by qualified special educators. One can only wonder what issues the future will bring as more and more children are served exclusively by regular educators who do not work under special education supervision and who are themselves responsible for providing whatever services the child needs.

The required statement of services to be provided is the most important and often the most neglected portion of the IEP. Services are typically described only by check marks on the face sheet of the IEP. For example, special education will be indicated only with a check mark next to "resource room" or by the word "consultation," etc. Even a cursory perusal of the several hundred IEP rulings which have been reported reveals a much broader and detailed view of specification of services is required.

The range of services that must be included on the IEP is indirectly defined by the fact that, unless state law requires more, each student is entitled only to a program that is reasonably calculated to allow benefit, not to a "best" or "most appropriate" program (*Hendrick Hudson Bd. v. Rowley*, 458 U.S. 176 (1982)). On the other hand, the scope of the services is also driven by the fact that all of the student's educational needs must be addressed. The scope of "education" in this context is very broad. It has been held to include self-esteem, coping skills to deal with rejection, feeding, gross motor activities, motor-sensory stimulation of a comatose student, self-help, vocational and prevocational skills, social skill development, organizational and attentional skills, academic tutoring, language, and much more. Rulings on related services have mandated assistive technology (e.g., auditory trainers, computers, spellers, wheelchairs), catheterization, parent and family counseling, extended school year, toileting assistance, special diets, interpreters, sign language training for parents, medical evaluation, occupational therapy, cognitive therapy, after-school aides, summer music programs, expressive therapy, early transportation to SAT review courses, music therapy, note-taking services, and much, much more including residential placements.

The amount of time to be committed to each of the various services must be appropriate to the child and included in the IEP in a way that is clear to all who develop and implement the IEP (1998 Appendix C, Question 32). OSEP has said that a range of times is not sufficient to indicate the necessary commitment of resources (*Ackron*, 17 EHLR 287 (OSEP, 1990)). This position appears to require an exact specification of minutes, hours, or other units appropriate to the service. One sad but foreseeable result of this policy is that often only a bare minimum of services is written into the IEP. Suppose a child is believed to need speech therapy for 30 minutes daily and the district is willing and able to provide that amount. Many district personnel believe they must provide every minute that is written and that if the student or therapist misses a day, is late, or if the school is closed for a snow day the district will "owe" the missed time and/or be "liable" for not providing the missed service. In fact, if there is an interruption in service one must look to the reason, the duration, and the effect on the student to determine whether it is a denial of an appropriate program (*Rockville (IN) Comm. Sch. Corp.*, EHLR 352.175 (OCR, 1986)). Since districts believe they cannot write an honest range, such as four to five sessions of 25-30 minutes weekly, they will specify the lowest that might be foreseeable, such as four 25-minute sessions weekly. That represents a loss of 50% (150 minutes versus 100 minutes) from what the district personnel believe is needed and are actually willing to provide. The use of reasonable ranges would seem to be a better practice, but it is clearly prohibited by OSEP.

Related Services

The test for whether a service is a "related" service that must be included on the IEP and provided at no expense to the parents is whether the service is necessary to enable the student to benefit from special education.

A hearing officer ruled, apparently mistakenly, that accommodations in the **regular** class need not be provided under the IDEA because related services, by definition, are limited to those necessary to benefit from **special education** (WI. SEA, S.D. *of Beloit*, 25 IDELR 109 (1996)). However, even if that were correct, all IDEA eligible students are also entitled to the protections of §504 and the Americans with Disabilities Act, both of which require such accommodations. The history teacher who was held liable for $15,000 damages for refusing to modify tests for a student with learning disabilities can also attest to the necessity of complying with needed modifications (*Doe v.Withers*, 20 IDELR 422 (W.VA. Cir. Ct., 1993)).

What is a related service for one student may not be for another. And what is a related service for a student at one point in time may not be later. A common error is to think that a particular service is or is not a related service and to overlook the fact that it depends upon student need. Another common mistake has been to think a student is entitled to a service if he or she can benefit from the service.

A difficult and potentially very expensive related service determination involves the distinction between **medical treatment** that need not be paid for by the district (or other public agency) and **health services** that must be paid for by the district. The U.S. Supreme Court has developed a two-part inquiry to determine whether a service is a related service which must be provided at no expense to the parents of a child with a disability:

1. Is the service "required to assist the child to benefit from special education"? If not, it is not a related service. If so, ask:

2. Is it excluded from IDEA coverage as a "medical service rendered for other than diagnostic or evaluative purposes" (*Irving Independent S.D. v. Tatro*, 468 U.S. 883 (1984))?

To answer this inquiry one must know what "medical service" means. In *Tatro*, the Court articulated a bright-line test which held that excluded medical services are "… services provided by a licensed physician" that serve other than diagnostic or evaluative purposes. The context of *Tatro* was the provision of clean intermittent catheterization, a relatively simple, inexpensive procedure which could be done by a trained aide. The question that has arisen in subsequent decisions is whether this excluded medical services definition of *Tatro* should be applied when the services, unlike catheterization, are complex, expensive, and risky. At the present time the courts are split as to whether *Tatro* applies to these cases. For example, *Detsel v. Auburn S.D.*, 820 F.2d. 587 (2nd Cir., 1987) rejected the *Tatro* rule and held that the exclusion of extensive, therapeutic health services (e.g., tracheotomy and gastrostomy, requiring the constant and undivided attention of a nurse) was "in keeping with the spirit" of the regulatory definition of related services and the district did not have to provide them.

Bevin H. v. Wright, 666 F.Supp. 71 (W.D. Pa., 1987) adopted the *Detsel* reasoning and cited the "private duty" nursing requirement (i.e., life threatening circumstances requiring constant attention) as distinguishing this case from *Tatro*. The court held that the "… nursing services required are so varied, intensive, and costly, and more in the nature of 'medical services' that they are not properly includable as 'related services.'"

However, *Macomb Co. v. Joshua S.*, 715 F.Supp. 824 (E.D. Mich., 1989) strenuously rejected *Detsel* and *Bevin* for departing from the *Tatro* analysis. *Macomb* found no basis to believe that states are free to decide on the basis of cost and effort which services are to be excluded. Therefore, the *Macomb* court relied simply and directly on *Tatro* and held the complex and expensive health services had to be provided at no cost to the parents.

Similarly, the 8th Circuit Court applied *Tatro* in a case involving bladder catheterization, suctioning of tracheotomy, ventilator setting checks, ambu bag administrations, blood pressure monitoring, and much more. The court held that these services did not require a doctor's attention and therefore, since the court was bound by *Tatro*'s bright-line test, the school was responsible under the IDEA for providing these related services (*Cedar Rapids Comm. S.D. v. Garret F.*, 106 F.3d 882 (8th Cir., 1997)).

Psychiatric Services. The 9th Circuit Court had to decide whether a placement in a psychiatric hospital was a related service or an excluded medical service. The court focused on the purpose for the placement and explicitly rejected the "licensed physician" criterion of *Tatro* as the sole criterion. The court also found that a program clearly aimed at curing a mental illness does not become a related service just because it can be implemented by staff other than physicians. This view raises difficult questions about most behavioral treatments for seriously emotionally disturbed children. The court specifically rejected the proposition that the IDEA requires schools to fund treatment for psychiatric illnesses (*Clovis Unified S.D. v. Cal. Office*, 903 F.2d. 635 (9th Cir., 1990)).

Not only do psychiatric placements pose these difficult medical treatment exclusion issues, but so do more simple therapeutic interventions which don't involve placement. Under *Clovis*, one must wonder whether, for example, behavioral therapy focused on reducing phobic or compulsive behavior would be excluded as "treatment for psychiatric illness." This is a difficult area. Nevertheless, three tentative rules have emerged:

1. Residential placements made for educational reasons (purposes) or made for "inextricably intertwined" medical-behavioral-educational reasons (purposes) are related services.

2. Residential placements made for medical reasons are not related services; however, a FAPE must be made available in or during that placement.

3. In determining whether psychotherapy, apart from the setting, is a related service, the *Tatro* rule of whether it must be provided by a licensed physician would seem to be applicable.

Extended School Year. Extended school year (ESY) services may also be required as a related service. The common ESY pattern is summer school, but extended days or services on the weekend are also possible. The IEP team has the authority to determine on an individual basis whether an ESY program is necessary. The most widely used test for entitlement is whether the ESY services are necessary to prevent undue regression and/or undue difficulty in regaining lost skills (*Armstrong v. Kline*, 513 F.Supp. 425 (E.D. Pa., 1980)), but this may be somewhat inappropriate, as discussed in Chapter Five.

Six common district sins related to the failure to offer and provide ESY were all flagrant in *Reusch v. Fountain*, 872 F.Supp. 1421 (D. Md., 1994). The court held these ESY practices all violate the IDEA:

    1. Failing to provide adequate notice regarding ESY to parents of disabled students.

2. Utilizing procedures that delay decisions regarding the providing of ESY to disabled students.

3. Making decisions on ESY too late in the school year.

4. Failing to address ESY at annual review meetings, and failing to document the required discussions of ESY.

5. Failing to apply a proper standard for the determination of whether students should receive ESY as part of their IEPs.

6. Failing to comply with requirements for an individualized program, including LRE considerations when ESY is offered.

Methodology

Teaching and related services "methodologies or approaches" are to be discussed and considered by the IEP team but are not expected to be written into the IEP (H. Rep. No. 105-95 (1997, pp. 100-101)). The distinction between these "methodologies or approaches" on the one hand and program modifications (which **must** be included on the IEP) on the other may be easier for lawyers to make than for educators.

Classroom Modifications

Classroom modifications are commonly made by regular education personnel with assistance, consultation, or monitoring by special educators. Modifications may be required in tests, texts, homework, assignments, grading, or more. By spelling these out in the IEP one can ensure that all necessary changes are made in a consistent way whenever and in whatever classes they are needed. (In the next chapters some practical tips for maximizing the appropriateness and helpfulness of these modifications are suggested.) Too often classroom modifications have not been addressed by IEP teams, sometimes because of the erroneous belief that the IEP team lacks the authority to require regular teachers to make changes.

The regular education teacher who is on the IEP team must help determine the classroom and program modifications, the needed supplementary aids and services, and necessary supports for school personnel (34 CFR 300.346(d)).

Transition Services

The 1997 IEP requirements emphasize preparing students with disabilities for post-school life, including employment, independent living, or formal education. To this end the requirements regarding transition needs and services are much more detailed than previously.

At Age 14

When a student with a disability reaches age 14, or younger if appropriate, the IEP must include "… a statement of the transition service **needs** [authors' emphasis] under the applicable IEP component such as advanced-placement courses or vocational education program" (34 CFR 300.347(b)(l)(i)). As Appendix C (1998) explains:

> …[B]eginning at age 14, the IEP team, in determining appropriate measurable annual goals (including benchmarks or short-term objectives) and services for a student, must determine what instruction and educational experiences will assist the student to prepare for transition from secondary education to post-secondary life. The statement of transition service needs should relate directly to the student's goals beyond secondary education, and show how planned studies are linked to these goals. For example, a student interested in exploring a career in computer science may have a statement of transition service needs connected to technology course work, while another student's statement of transition needs could describe why public bus transportation training is important for future independence in the community. Though the focus of the transition planning process may shift as the student approaches graduation, the IEP team must discuss specific areas beginning at the age of 14 years and review these areas annually (Question 11).

At Age 16

By age 16, or younger if appropriate, IEPs must address needed transition **services** (in contrast to **needs** at age 14) and if appropriate a statement of interagency responsibilities or linkage. Transition services is defined as a coordinated set of activities that:

> (a) Is designed within an outcome-oriented process, that promotes movement from school to post-school activities, including post-secondary education, vocational training, integrated employment (including supported employment), continuing and adult education, adult services, independent living, or community participation;
>
> (b) Is based on the individual student's needs, taking into account the student's preferences and interests; and

(c) Includes

    (1) Instruction;

    (2) Related services;

    (3) Community experiences;

    (4) The development of employment and other post-school adult living objectives; and

    (5) If appropriate, acquisition of daily living skills and functional vocational evaluation (34 CFR 300.27).

If the IEP team determines that instruction, related services, community experiences, or employment and other adult living objectives aren't necessary, the IEP must include that determination and details about how it was made.

Much confusion has arisen over the exact role of the school with regard to other agencies that are to be involved in providing or paying for transition services. First, the school must invite a representative of such an agency. If the agency doesn't send someone, then the school must take other steps to get that agency to participate in planning (34 CFR 300.344(B)(3)).

If another agency fails to provide agreed-upon transition services then the school, consistent with being the ultimately responsible agency (the Harry Truman "the buck stops here" place), must initiate a meeting to examine the transition goals and perhaps to revise the IEP (34 CFR 300.348(a)). Appendix C (1998) elaborates:

> This interagency planning and coordination may be supported through a variety of mechanisms, including memoranda of understanding, interagency agreements, assignment of a transition coordinator to work with other participating agencies, or the establishment of guidelines to work with other agencies identified as potential service providers. If an agreed-upon service by another agency is not provided, the public agency responsible for the student must exercise alternative strategies to meet the student's needs. This requires that the public agency provide the services, or convene an IEP meeting as soon as possible to identify alternative strategies to meet the needs of the transition service needs of the student, and to revise the IEP accordingly. Alternative strategies might include the identification of another funding source, referral to another agency, the public agency's identification of other district-wide or community resources that it can use to meet the student's identified need appropriately, or a combination of these strategies... (Question 12).

Nothing in the IDEA excuses any other agency of its responsibilities to provide transition services, but the bottom line is that the school district still must ensure that the student has FAPE available, one way or another. And since the "F" in FAPE stands for "free to the parent" the district might end up paying a private organization to provide a transition service another state or Federal agency was supposed to, but failed to provide.

Two 1994 due process hearings against an Iowa district resulted in rulings that the district's failure to provide appropriate transition planning and services precluded the district from graduating the students and obligated it to provide further vocational programs (IA. SEA, *Mason City Comm. S.D.*, 21 IDELR 241 (1994); IA. SEA, *Mason City Comm. S.D.*, 21 IDELR 248 (1994)).

A Federal court in South Dakota also evaluated all too common district transition practices. In this case the district believed it:

> … fulfills its responsibility to develop and implement interagency participation in transition services if it communicates to the disabled student and her parents the kinds of agencies in the community that may be able to help the student in the future and provides the student and her family with a "linkage" to those agencies (*Yankton S.D. v. Schramm*, 900 F.Supp. 1182 (D.S.D., 1995)).

Specifically, the transition plan adopted for this college bound student who had orthopedic disabilities stated that:

> … vocational rehabilitation services, Supplemental Security Income, and "other programs available" were explained and that Tracy will need "Public and private transportation with assistive devices when appropriate." The District wrote that, "If Tracy is eligible for SSI he [sic] will also be eligible for Medicaid," and that "Prairie Freedom Center will be contacted by Angie Schramm." In the block for "Advocacy and Legal Services," the District wrote, "Not applicable." In the remaining areas of "Personal Management and Family Relationship," "Financial and Income," "Living Arrangements," "Leisure and Recreation," and "Medical Services and Resources," the district provided no other transition planning. Tracy and her parents were assigned follow-up responsibility in every area with [two] exceptions … (*Ibid*).

The court declared quite simply and directly that "… such a minimal approach to school district responsibility for transition services … fails to comport" with the IDEA and that their transition plan does not satisfy any of the legal mandates. The district's failure to understand its own responsibilities caused it to fail to inform the family adequately of the nature and scope of transition services available.

Nonparticipation With Nondisabled

Previously, IEPs addressed the amount of time a child with a disability would participate in the regular class. The new requirement (34 CFR 300.347 (a)(4)) is to explain the extent, if any, to which the child will not participate with nondisabled children. This appears to be a broad requirement covering all aspects of the child's day.

Assessment Status

Concern has abounded that special education students were not being vigorously assessed and held accountable in state- or district-wide testing and/or that when they were included in such assessments their scores were not included nor reported. The solution is the requirement (34 CFR 300.347 (a)(5)) to address this assessment in the IEP and for the team to determine whether and how the assessment will be done. Measurement experts will be busy for a long time deciding how to report and otherwise treat test scores that result from testing modifications.

Progress Reporting

The movement toward greater accountability in special education has resulted in the requirement (34 CFR 300.347 (a)(7)) of student progress reporting to parents, in addition to any that was done before. Not only must the amount of progress be reported at least as often as to parents of nondisabled students, but a calculation must be shared as to whether that rate of progress is sufficient to enable the student to reach the annual goal.

Behavioral Plan

Whenever a student's behavior impedes his or her own learning or that of others, and whenever discipline beyond ten days of suspension occurs, functional assessment of behavior must be conducted and a behavioral plan developed. If this has previously been done and included in the IEP it must be reevaluated and revised. Very simply, one must now deal programmatically, not just punitively, with inappropriate conduct and this must be shown in the IEP (34 CFR 300.346 (a)(2)(i); 34 CFR 300.520 (b)(1)). The child's actual or potential regular education teacher who is now a mandated member of the IEP team must, to the extent appropriate, assist in the team's determination of the positive behavioral interventions and strategies for a child whose behavior interferes with learning (34 CFR 300.346 (a)(2)(i); 34 CFR 300.520 (b)(1)).

English as a Second Language (ESL) Needs

While a child may not be identified as disabled because of English being his or her second language, some children who are disabled also have special needs arising from their ESL status. These needs must be considered and addressed, as they relate to the rest of the IEP (34 CFR 300.346 (a)(2)(ii)).

Braille

In recent years many children who need to be proficient in Braille have not been taught this skill. The new, explicit requirement of the IDEA (34 CFR 300.346 (a)(2)(iii)) requires the IEP team to evaluate the child's reading and writing skills and needs, present and future, and provide Braille instruction unless it is not appropriate.

Communication Needs

Many lawsuits have arisen when parents of a deaf child wanted a different language for their child than the school was prepared to offer. The typical judicial resolution has been to say this is an issue of methodology and therefore the school may do whatever it chooses, regardless of the family's or child's needs or preference or status. The new regulation (34 CFR 300.346 (a)(2)(iv)) appears to require a consideration by the district of factors about the child, not just about the language instruction the district has available. This could signal a most welcome change.

Assistive Technology

Assistive technology must be included in the IEP and provided to a student when it is a necessary part of his or her special education or related services or supplementary aids and services (*Letter to anonymous*, 24 IDELR 854 (OSEP, 1996)). Districts need not provide assistive technology if the device or service is required regardless of whether the student attends school. This exclusion does not apply, however, if the device or service is necessary to allow the student to receive FAPE and is part of the student's special education, related services, or supplementary aids and services (*Letter to anonymous*, 24 IDELR 388 (OSEP, 1996)).

An assistive technology device is broadly defined in the IDEA as:

> … any item, piece of equipment, or product system, whether acquired commercially off the shelf, modified, or customized, that is used to increase, maintain, or improve the functional capabilities of a child with a disability (34 CFR 300.5).

An assistive technology service means:

> … any service that directly assists a child with a disability in the selection, acquisition, or use of an assistive technology device. The term includes

> (a) The evaluation of the needs of a child with a disability, including a functional evaluation of the child in the child's customary environment;

> (b) Purchasing, leasing, or otherwise providing for the acquisition of assistive technology devices by children with disabilities;

> (c) Selecting, designing, fitting, customizing, adapting, applying, maintaining, repairing, or replacing assistive technology devices;

> (d) Coordinating and using other therapies, interventions, or services with assistive technology devices, such as those associated with existing education and rehabilitation plans and programs;

> (e) Training or technical assistance for a child with a disability or, if appropriate, that child's family; and

> (f) Training or technical assistance for professionals (including individuals providing education or rehabilitation services), employers, or other individuals who provide services to, employ, or are otherwise substantially involved in the major life functions of that child (34 CFR 300.6).

IEP Forms and Computers

In too many IEP meetings someone asks at least once, "Where do we put this on the form?" Forms by their nature tend to interfere with true individualization. The fewer lines and pre-shaped spaces a form has, the more likely one can readily use the form. That is the primary reason we recommend one of the IEP "Non-Forms." (More will be said about these forms and their use in Chapter Four.) It is important to reiterate that a proper form will contain all the required elements in the simplest way possible, allowing for the most flexibility and creativity. If a state or a district has come to require more on the IEP form than the IDEA regulations require, it would be best to go back to the basics. This is definitely a time and place where simpler is better.

Computers are being widely used to assist in the "paper work" of IEPs. In the two rulings located, computer generation of the IEP was found to result in a failure of individualization and therefore it violated FAPE (*Rockford, Ill. S.D. #205*, EHLR 352:465 (OCR, 1987); MASS. SEA, *Aaron S. v. Westford Pub. Sch.*, EHLR 509:122 (1987)).

The use of computers for management of IEPs, review dates, etc. is clearly appropriate and is not to be confused with their more questionable use to generate descriptions of "unique" needs, present levels of performance, services, and goals and objectives. It is the latter use that raises serious questions about true individualization. The supporters of the use of computers suggest that the writing of behavioral objectives is at best difficult, and it is. So, they reason, if the need, the service, and the annual goal have been developed solely and uniquely for that child, is it not then appropriate to use a computerized bank of objectives for that goal? Perhaps, but not necessarily. First, remember that only two or three objectives are anticipated for each goal. Second, doesn't one expect different children to progress at different rates? Shouldn't the answer to the question of "How far, by when?" be as individualized as all the rest? The short answer to the computer issue may be that if "it" can be efficiently generated by computer, "it" may not need to be on the IEP. Remember, too, that IEPs are to be developed by teachers, a parent, an evaluation expert, and a district representative who seldom has any special education expertise. One must think ever so carefully about what the IEP is supposed to be.

A closely related issue is that of pre-printed IEP objectives. Here is the clear and simple conclusion of one hearing officer about them:

> The 1995-96 IEP is in violation of regulations. The goals and objectives in reading, writing, and spelling are a series of pre-printed statements which were, as related by the special education teacher's testimony, used for all students in the group with J. They were not designed to meet J's individual needs (ME. SEA, *Schoodic Comm. S.D.*, 26 IDELR 219 (1997)).

Of all the "mass production" IEP form problems, none is any more revealing of nonindividualization than short-term objective statements with a blank to be filled in with a percentage of mastery, e.g., the student will comprehend _____% of the social science concepts. This example is vague, meaningless, not measurable, and not truly individualized. Furthermore, if one examined either a student's last year's IEP or that teacher's other students' IEPs for this year, a safe bet would be the percentages would barely vary. Eighty percent is a favorite, regardless of the task, e.g., the student will interact appropriately 80% of the time. Sometimes the same pre-printed goals and objectives will be used year after year with only the percentage of mastery changing. Typically they start at 70% and increase five per-cent per year, regardless of how nonsensical that may be. Mass produced IEP goals and objectives are not responsive to students' **unique** educational needs, by definition. Nor are they legal or appropriate. Other than that ….

Confidentiality of IEPs

In the past, many teachers, especially at the secondary level, reported they had no idea which of their students, if any, had IEPs and that they never saw the IEP even when they were informed that a student had one.

The IDEA regulations now make it clear that all of a child's teachers are to receive a copy of the IEP (34 CFR 300.344, Note). This is as it should be. By its very na-ture a good IEP is always helpful and sometimes essential in providing an appro-priate program for the student. Rarely is a student's disability so mild or limited that he or she requires no modifications or accommodations in regular junior high/middle school or high school classes.

When the practice of hiding IEPs from teachers was questioned the common an-swer was the belief that confidentiality would be violated if IEPs were shared. While it is true IEPs are education records and must be treated as such, the Family Educational Rights and Privacy Act (FERPA) has an exception which is pertinent. Under Reg. 99.31(a) of the FERPA regulations, an educational agency **may** disclose personally identifiable information from the education records of a student without the written consent of the parents "… if the disclosure is to other school officials, including teachers, within the educational institution or local edu-cational agency who have been determined by the agency or institution to have le-gitimate educational interests" in that information.

In the event that there is a state or district confidentiality requirement that ap-pears to prohibit the sharing of IEPs there are at least two solutions. The first is simply to obtain parental permission to do so. Parents should insist that all teachers have copies of their children's IEPs, even if they have to provide them themselves. The second is to recognize that superseding Federal law requires the distribution of IEP's. Of course it should go without saying that the IEP should not contain any information beyond what is required. It would not be appropriate, for example, to include the student's category of disability or intelligence test score.

The IEP Big Picture and Bottom Line

At least five general principles clearly emerge from a review of the hundreds of past IEP rulings from agencies and courts:

1. **All** of a child's **unique** needs arising from the disability must be addressed, not just his or her academic needs (e.g., *Russell v. Jefferson S.D.*, 609 F.Supp. 605 (N.D. CA, 1985); *Abrahamson v. Hershman*, 701 F.2d 223 (1st Cir., 1983)).

2. The **availability of services may not be considered** in writing the IEP. If a service is needed it must be written on the IEP and if the district does not have it available, it must be provided by another agency. One of the earliest of all the agency rulings mandated that availability of services be disregarded in writing the IEP (*Leconte*, EHLR 211:146 (OSEP, 1979)). This principle has been reiterated repeatedly, but virtually ignored by the field.

3. The IEP is a firm, **legally binding commitment** of resources. The district must provide the services described or the IEP must be amended (*Beck*, EHLR 211:145 (OSEP, 1979)).

4. IEPs must be **individualized**. They must be developed to fit the unique needs of the child, not to describe a predetermined program. The same amounts of therapy on many IEPs (e.g., every child who receives speech therapy in a particular building receives 30 minutes daily) also reveals a violation of this individualization requirement (*Tucson, AZ Unified S.D. #1*, EHLR 352:547 (OCR, 1987)).

5. All of the **components** of the IEP must be present as required by 34 CFR 300.347, e.g., measurable goals and objectives and specific special education and related services.

If in addition to following these five content principles one also ensures the procedural essentials of IEP development the result will be an IEP that provides FAPE to the child. The law requires no more and no less.

Now that we've looked at the legal requirements within which the IEP process must operate we can move on, in the next chapter, to talk about how **not** to write IEPs.

Empty, Not Serious, and Other Wrong-Headed IEPs

Sadly, most IEPs are horrendously burdensome to teachers and nearly useless to parents and children. Far from being a creative, flexible, data-based, and individualized application of the best of educational interventions to a child with unique needs, the typical IEP is "empty," devoid of specific services to be provided. It says what the IEP team hopes the student will be able to accomplish, but little if anything about the special education interventions and the related services or the classroom modifications that will enable him or her to reach those goals. Typically, the IEP team begins and ends its efforts with goals and objectives for the student to accomplish. For example, one actual IEP said merely, "Tim will improve his behavior 75% of the time." Apart from the other problems inherent in this slaughtering of behavioral language and concepts, we see the "empty IEP"—nothing is said about **what the district will do** to teach Tim to change his behavior for the better. All the responsibility is on Tim. Clearly, there is no intention of taking this one goal-objective seriously, that is, of using it to evaluate how well the program is working. Many if not most goals and objectives couldn't be measured if one tried, and all too often no effort is made to actually assess the child's progress toward the goal.

The Real World

The real world of public school IEPs, teachers, students, and their parents seems nearly untouched by the academic world of educational interventions. Parents are busy struggling, for example, to force districts to grant graduation credit for resource room English, to include decoding goals on the IEP even though the school uses whole language, to obtain individual language therapy instead of group speech therapy, to prevent the student's threatened or impending illegal expulsion, to ensure the IEP is implemented once it is written, to get the regular teachers to accept the need for shorter spelling lists and oral reports and tests, and to get keyboarding instruction instead of bare computer time written into the IEP.

Special educators want to know, for example, how to cut down on paper work, if it is legally correct to bring a completed IEP to the meeting, what happens if they tell the parent the child really does need a tutor, how to get the regular teacher to come to the IEP meeting, and if a caseload of 70 resource room students is legal.

The IEPs themselves often reflect currently available and ongoing instructional programs and packages, not the individual students' needs. They reflect available services, not needed services. They are not individualized and they are often not taken seriously. Some are never looked at, many are only partially implemented, and most are not distributed to all the teachers who work with the students.

How did it come about that IEPs are often such a far cry from what they could be? It began with the practice of the last many decades in which the basic special education procedure was to identify the child by category of disability (e.g., mental retardation), and then place the child strictly by that disability category, i.e., place him or her in a program for mentally retarded children. The assumption was that appropriate programs had been developed for each type of disability and that those appropriate programs were implemented in placements designated by disability category. Barsch (1968) described this three decades ago:

> Educators of the deaf, blind, physically handicapped, emotionally disturbed, trainable and educable mentally retarded have spent many years developing specifically defined curricula to meet the educational needs of these different groups of children. These curricula have a well-established rationale and, for the most part, are enacted by teachers in a high degree of comfort. A great deal is known about effective teaching methods and techniques for each of these groups (p. 15).

When the IDEA went into effect in 1977 (then called the Education of All Handicapped Children Act) educators did the predictable human thing and changed their practice as little as possible. They added IEPs to "business as usual." They labeled a child eligible, decided on placement, and then made the teacher write up one more IEP version of the ongoing program in that placement. This basic erroneous and illegal framework has been fostered and upheld by a network of other questionable and/or illegal practices, such as: computer generation of stock

IEPs; refusal to include needed regular class modifications on the IEP; failure to base related services on children's needs rather than on cost or availability; failure to base placement decisions on previously completed IEPs; failure to include a qualified district representative on every IEP team; failure to ensure full, equal, and meaningful parental participation on every IEP team; failure to address all the child's unique characteristics/needs and instead focusing almost exclusively on academic goals; failure to specify and describe the services to be provided; and the list goes on and on.

When educators tried to incorporate IEPs into the old framework they did it by a sequential process:

1. They labeled the eligible child by disability category, e.g., Amy is orthopedically impaired.

2. They placed Amy into a program for that disability.

3. They required the teacher to write up (or down) one more rendition of that ongoing program and called it Amy's IEP, even though the program went on as it was whether Amy was in it or not.

What the law has actually required since 1977 is also a three-step process, but with critical differences. The mandated, correct process is:

1. One **must** determine whether the child is eligible for an IEP.

2. One **must** individually examine and specify the child's needs and the services to be provided (i.e., one must develop the IEP).

3. One **must** place the child in the least restrictive environment in which an appropriate program can be provided and the child's education can be achieved satisfactorily.

Graphically, the old way looks like that shown in Figure 7:

Figure 7

The Wrong Way

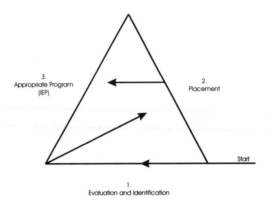

And the IDEA way looks like that shown in Figure 8:

Figure 8

The Right Way

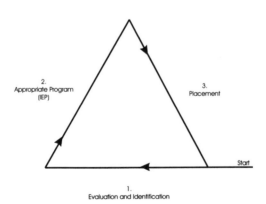

(And yes, this diagram has appeared before. It is **important**!)

It was more than understandable that educators would attempt to implement the then new law with as little change in practice as possible. It was downright predictable, human nature being as it is.

Fully recognizing the difference between the old way and the IDEA way is crucial to improving IEPs. For many, the old way is deeply ingrained and it seems practical. And so, once more, and for the last time, we look at the wrong way: One has maintained the old ways and said, for example, "Joe is learning disabled, so we'll put him in the resource room for learning disabled students and then have the resource teacher write up one more copy of the ongoing program in that room and call it the IEP." Instead, one should have said, "Joe is eligible, Joe's individual needs are X, Y, Z, and can be met by services A, B, C (his IEP) which we can implement in placement P." Districts have tried to fit children into programs, just as has long been done, rather than flexibly and creatively designing new programs, one child at a time.

The even more trendy version of the old, wrong way is to say, for example, "Jim is eligible and he has to be in a regular class (no, he doesn't, but that's another story) and we use a consultation model so that's what his IEP will say." Jim's needs have been overlooked and the existing delivery system has been the tail that wagged the dog, again.

And, not for the last time, what the IDEA now requires is: (1) the evaluation and identification of an eligible student; (2) the development of a truly individualized education program (IEP), without regard to the category of disability or the availability of services; and (3) an individual placement decision based upon the IEP, not on the disability or administrative convenience.

Before we leave the real world and head toward better IEPs we'll take one further glance at some frequently occurring problems in the old-style IEPs.

Common Problems in Real-World IEPs

Is there really any point in looking at not-so-perfect IEPs or parts of IEPs? Absolutely! It provides an opportunity to demonstrate how common practices go astray from the letter and spirit of the law. Following we will examine some typical IEP problems. Each illustrates misconceptions or practices that must be reevaluated before one can start over on the road to better IEPs.

Problematic Statements of Needs and
Present Levels of Performance

All the child's unique educational needs resulting from the disability must be spelled out. Whether or not a clear, precise, explicit listing of needs on the IEP is a legal requirement, it is surely a best practice, and the IDEA does expressly require a description of how the disability affects the child's involvement and progress in the general curriculum. Too many IEPs contain little or no specification of needs. The fear is that if a need is mentioned in the IEP, it will have to be addressed. Right! It will and it must be. If Barry, for example, needs one-to-one tutoring in a quiet room, that need must be on the IEP, and the corresponding service must be provided. Remember, when an ostrich "hides" with its head on the sand its tail end is more than a little vulnerable. (An ostrich puts its head on, not in the sand, true.)

Present levels of performance (PLOPs) are the beginning point from which the child's progress must be measured. Every annual goal must itself be measurable and the PLOP is the measurable starting point on the journey toward the goal. There must be a PLOP for every goal.

The bottom line is that **all needs** must be addressed by a service and/or a goal. And a present level of performance and goal must be specified for all instructional services. Pitfalls to be avoided include:

1. Omitting a critical need, e.g., failing to state that Pamela is highly allergic to scents and therefore failing to provide the needed service of a scent-free environment.

2. Using the category of eligibility as a PLOP, e.g., "Todd has a learning disability in reading and language."

3. Stating only a vague PLOP, such as, "Jenna is deficient in keyboarding," rather than stating it in measurable terms. When instruction is the needed service, as here, a measurable PLOP and goal are required.

Problematic Statements of Special Services and Modifications

Sins of omission prevail in the vital portion of the IEP specifying the services for the child. Not only does the law require a **statement** of the special education and related services, supplementary aids and services, program modifications, and personnel support the child needs, but it also requires a beginning date, frequency, location, and duration for each.

IEPs commonly have omitted such statements altogether and have instead provided only a check mark and no descriptive statement or a statement so vague as to prevent one from determining whether the needed service was or was not provided. Here are typical **too vague** or **too general** service descriptions: reading remediation, community trips for independent living skills, tutoring in math, modification of the curriculum, special education teacher/aide, social skill training, a crisis management plan, daily academic instruction, an educational assistant will provide training, the school counselor will assist in exploring college options, the teacher will work with the student on the computer, etc. Vague and general as these are, they are one tiny step above a printed list of services waiting for a check mark.

Complete descriptions of services that all allow meaningful determinations of when the service is being provided and that therefore constitute an enforceable commitment of district resources will appear in Chapter Four. For now, here is one example: One-to-one direct instruction in color, shape, and spatial concepts by the classroom teacher for 15 minutes per day in the classroom beginning Sept. 1, 1999 until Sept. 1, 2000.

Problematic Goals and Objectives

Several common problems in writing annual goals and short-term objectives are presented next. Unfortunately, there are more than these, but these illustrate several critical points.

A Not-So-Wonderful Goal: Insufficient Progress Projected

Jerry will improve his reading by six months on a standardized test such as the Woodcock-Johnson (W-J).

Comment. Six months (or even a year) would not begin to get a learning disabled student caught up to his ability level, assuming he is substantially behind. There is a most troublesome trend now whereby too many professionals are confusing learning disabilities with mental retardation. Many children who need reading goals on their IEPs are learning disabled, not mentally retarded. By definition, research, and experience, it is known that learning disabled children **can** learn to read at or near their ability level, i.e., they can catch up if they are taught effectively. For almost all children who have learning disabilities, a systematic, highly structured, synthetic phonics based method of teaching reading is essential. Among such reading programs with strong databases demonstrating their effectiveness are those of Orton-Gillingham, Slingerland, Herman, Wilson, Spalding, Lindamood-Bell, Reading Mastery, Alphabetic Phonics, and Project Read. All these and all other highly effective reading programs require specific and thorough teacher training to a defined level of expertise. Perhaps that is why so many public schools resist these programs and prefer the "mix children with print and stir lightly" osmotic and other noninstructional approaches to teaching reading.

To define a proper annual goal in reading for a learning disabled student, given an appropriate and effective methodology, first determine how long it would take a skilled teacher to get the student to grade level and then project progress on a fairly straight line basis. Let us say, for example, one has a sixth grade student with average intellectual ability who reads at a third grade level. The teacher says that in two years the student can be at grade level. That is, by eighth grade, he'll be at eighth grade level. He has five years of work to make up in two years, so the projection would be about two or two and a half years' gain in sixth grade.

A Not-So-Wonderful Goal: Misuse of Percentages

Karen will improve her handwriting by 80%.

Comment. One gets the general idea readily—Karen has a need for better writing and total perfection is not expected immediately. However, writing IEPs isn't playing horseshoes and this just doesn't get close enough. Percentages seem to be worshiped unduly, although they can have some legitimate uses in goals and objectives. For example, to strive for 90% of spelling words to be written correctly on the first weekly test might be quite appropriate. However, to accept only 90% of the words in a reading passage to be decoded accurately is to accept an error rate which grossly interferes with comprehension. Similarly, if 80% of the words in an essay were legible, one of five would **not** be legible. That is not an acceptable target.

Even more glaring is the misuse of percentages in goals related to behavior. One memorable IEP from a small town in western Oregon projected that, "Levi will have acceptable behavior 80% of the time." Can you imagine what it would be like to be around someone whose behavior was unacceptable 20% of the time?

And to think that was the goal! Bad enough if it had been Levi's present level of performance.

A Not-So-Wonderful Goal: Misuse of Percentages

Given a short paragraph, James will be able to identify the main idea with 95% accuracy.

Comment. Exactly how does one identify a main idea with 95% accuracy? Does this mean that if James were given 100 short paragraphs he would correctly identify the main idea in 95 of them? Or that given one he would almost accurately (but not quite) identify the main idea? The old rule of editing applies here—if in doubt, delete. Better to say that James will be able to identify the main idea in a short paragraph at his reading level.

A Not-So-Wonderful Goal: The Student Will "Choose"

Joshua will choose to be responsible for his own behavior. If he fails to do this, his parents will be called to remove him for the remainder of the day.

Comment. If the only specific special education and related services to be provided are check marks on the IEP face sheet, this "choose" language is especially apt to sound empty. Of course, this particular goal/objective statement is also too vague. People who frame objectives in terms of "the student will choose" to do or not do usually have a strong philosophical reason for choosing that language. However, that language poses the "empty" IEP problem in that it appears as if the district's sole contribution to the improved behavior may be its expectation that Joshua will choose to do better.

If a student who has an IEP has behavioral-social-emotional needs, they must be addressed by services on the IEP. Any time it is known or there is reason to suspect a child will have trouble with discipline, then discipline must be included. It is not the case that only children who are labeled seriously emotionally disturbed or emotionally or behaviorally disabled, etc. should have behavioral components in their IEPs. Nor is it true that a "behavioral IEP" is different in any way from any other. It may be most helpful to think in terms of a behavioral component, just as there might be an arithmetic component in an IEP.

Too often, parents will be requested or pressured to accept some responsibility through the IEP. This may range from providing a study space to removing the child from school. There is **no** authority or power in the IEP process to require **anything** of parents. The law is about what the district must do, not what parents must do. Parental cooperation is helpful in the extreme, beyond any doubt. The point is just that the IEP is not the place to formalize that cooperative working relationship.

The particular parental involvement suggested in Joshua's goal is a transparent and legally unacceptable way to avoid calling suspension what it is. The law has placed stringent limitations on the extent and the manner of suspensions and it is impossible to evade these by pretending that suspension isn't suspension, or that disciplinary removal from school is consistent with providing FAPE.

The whole area of discipline of students who have disabilities is complicated and difficult. A major principle that emerges from case law is that educators are expected to treat inappropriate behavior in a programmatic way, not just by exclusion from school. Another very important principle is that it is not appropriate to punish a student for behavior caused by the disability. If a deaf student fails to hear a teacher's request or if a blind kindergartner knocks down another child's block stack punishment is not even considered as the proper response. The appropriate response is less clear when a student diagnosed as severely emotionally disturbed because of violent, unprovoked aggression and hostility then continues that same pattern. A professional determination must be made as to whether the misconduct was caused by the disability. If it is, the IDEA requires a program change or change in placement rather than discipline per se.

While an in-depth examination of the issues involved in disciplining special education students is beyond our discussion, Figure 3 in Chapter One does provide a helpful flow chart and overview of the basic discipline procedures required by the IDEA.

A Not-So-Wonderful Goal: It Is Unnecessary

Given a blank map, Pat will label the continents and the major oceans with 90% accuracy.

Comment. Many goal/objective statements are similar to this one. They immediately trigger the question of whether they are really special education. Does such a goal/objective, legitimate as it may be, need to be on the IEP? If one recalls that only special education need be dealt with on the IEP, that by definition special education is specially designed instruction to meet a student's unique needs, and that it must be delivered by certified special educators or by aides working under direct supervision, it seems likely that this social studies goal need not be included. If the student was blind and the map was a relief map to be labeled in Braille, perhaps this goal would be closer to being special education. If the student was 21 years old, had moderate mental retardation, and was doing this exercise as part of a "travel in the community" unit preparatory to learning to ride the bus, perhaps it would be addressing a unique need. However, even that leaves the question of whether it would be "specially designed instruction." The very same questions can be raised about objectives such as, "Given ten fraction problems with mixed fractions, Pat will be able to add, subtract, multiply, and divide correctly nine out of ten times."

Here is what one hearing officer said about various IEP goals prepared for a special education student:

> ... [E]ach of [the] student's IEPs were so general that it would be difficult to believe the goals were even written for a special education student. For example:

> ... will improve math assignments ... will be able to complete story problems ... will identify the process to use in solving word problems correctly ... will complete lessons dealing with algebra and geometry ... will complete grade level math assignments, but at her own pace ... will complete grade level math tests ... will bring all materials needed to study periods ... will develop a positive, hardworking attitude to understand the relationship between forces, motion, and energy ... to understand American history from 1790-1865 ....

> These IEP examples clearly do not meet the *Rowley* threshold of providing personalized instruction to permit a child to benefit educationally (SEA MN., *Independent S.D. #204 Kasson-Mantorville*, 22 IDELR 380 (1994)).

A Not-So-Wonderful Goal: Vague, Meaningless, and/or Not Measurable

Rebecca will increase her active listening skills.

Comment. Other inadequate goals from the same IEP include "…[she] will increase auditory sequencing skills, auditory memory skills, active communication skills with peers, organizational skills, and written expression skills" (SEA MN, *Independent S.D. #283, St. Louis Park*, 22 IDELR 47 (1994)). Goals must include an expected ending level so that an observer can readily determine whether that level was or was not reached. If one says, for example, by the end of the year Zack will weigh no more than 140 pounds, the observer can readily determine success. But if the goal were simply to "lose weight" the observer would be unable, without more, to ascertain whether the goal had been accomplished.

These five common problems in IEP goals—**insufficient progress projected; misuse of percentages; "student will choose" language; including regular curriculum goals instead of special education goals; and vague, meaningless, and/or not measurable goals**—are frequently intertwined. One needs to avoid each and every one. The following IEPs further illustrate these and other problems.

Real-World Problematic IEPs

The IEPs and partial IEPs presented following are all real. They come from schools in several states, so the formats differ from one another. Our focus is **only** on the essentials of the IEP—the PLOPs, the services, and the goals/objectives—and the closeness of the sequential fit among them, moving from PLOP to service to goals and objectives.

Tammy

Tammy is an 11th grader who has cerebral palsy. She functions academically at a third to sixth grade equivalent level. Her speech is about 65% intelligible; she responds with one- or two-word phrases or by pointing. She presents no behavioral problems, is quiet in class, and responds to some humor by smiling. Her IEP consisted of ten pages of content area objectives in English, study skills, consumer education, math, and state history. Three selected pages are shown in Figures 9-11.

Figure 9
Tammy

INDIVIDUALIZED EDUCATION PROGRAM

Name ___ Tammy ___

Subject Area/Related Service ___ English Phase III ___

☐ Diploma   ☐ Certificate

Monitoring Teacher: ___

Method of Evaluation
1 - Tests
2 - Observation, Records
3 - Daily work
4 - Other ___

Evaluation Code
NP - No Progress: No gains or improvement
P - Progressing: Shows gains in learning the objective
M - Mastered: Has learned the skills for the objective
NA - Not Applicable: Objective not yet covered

Annual Goal Number	Short Term Objective(s)	Method of Eval.	Evaluation				Comments
			1QT	2QT	3QT	4QT	
1c To improve literature awareness	1. Given a short story in American literature in VHS presentation form, Tammy will identify the conflict, state how it is resolved, and justify her statements by citing from the tape with at least _75%_ accuracy.	2,3					Summer School 1c
1d To improve language study skills	1. Given 2 examples of personal views, Tammy will read or listen to the language used and explain what cultural beliefs, values, and/or interests are being reflected, and support her answer by citing from the examples given with _75%_ accuracy.	2,3					Summer School 1d
1e To improve oral communication	1. Tammy will use complete sentences and explain her ideas in a logical sequence (without pointing) with at least _80%_ accuracy, _75%_ of the time.	2,3					Summer School 1e

Figure 10
Tammy

INDIVIDUALIZED EDUCATION PROGRAM

Name: Tammy

Subject Area/Related Service: Study Skills

☐ Diploma ☐ Certificate

Monitoring Teacher: _____

Method of Evaluation
1 - Tests
2 - Observation, Records
3 - Daily work
4 - Other _____

Evaluation Code
NP - No Progress: No gains or improvement
P - Progressing: Shows gains in learning the objective
M - Mastered: Has learned the skills for the objective
NA - Not Applicable: Objective not yet covered

Annual Goal Number	Short Term Objective(s)	Method of Eval.	1QT	2QT	3QT	4QT	Comments
a	To improve basic and other life skills	Given activities and exercises in the following workbook-texts, *Getting Smarter: The Study Skills Improvement Program*, Tammy will in written form or oral evaluation, establish or demonstrate the following objectives:						Summer School 2a
		1. Tammy will improve her current study habits using her workbook-texts with 75% accuracy.	1,2,3					
		2. Tammy will improve her organizational skills by giving 6 examples pertinent to organizing her work, assignments, and homework with 75% accuracy.	1,2,3					
		3. Tammy will give 7 effective examples of how to budget a given time period, including 6 steps on designing her own schedule with 75% accuracy.	1,2,3					
		4. Tammy will examine priorities and goals and list 3 examples of long-term, short-term, weekly, and daily goals with 75% accuracy.	1,2,3					
		5. Tammy will improve her reading comprehension within an instructional range of 3.0 to 5.0 reading levels with 75% accuracy.	1,2,3					
		6. Tammy will improve her note-taking skills using a given outline format, identifying the main ideas with 75% accuracy.	1,2,3					
		7. To improve testing techniques, Tammy will state the 2 steps for test preparation.	1,2,3					

Figure 11
Tammy

INDIVIDUALIZED EDUCATION PROGRAM

Name ___Tammy___

Subject Area/Related Service ___Consumer Education___

☐ Diploma   ☐ Certificate

Monitoring Teacher: _____

Method of Evaluation
1 - Tests
2 - Observation, Records
3 - Daily work
4 - Other

Evaluation Code
NP - No Progress: No gains or improvement
P - Progressing: Shows gains in learning the objective
M - Mastered: Has learned the skills for the objective
NA - Not Applicable: Objective not yet covered

Annual Goal Number	Short Term Objective(s)	Method of Eval.	Evaluation				Comments
			1QT	2QT	3QT	4QT	
To understand the value of money and the importance of money	1. Tammy will create a sound budget when given a hypothetical financial situation with _75%_ accuracy.	1,2,3					Summer School 2J
	2. Tammy will spell, define, and use 10 vocabulary words per chapter/unit, pertinent to banking and money management with _75%_ accuracy.	1,2,3					

Needs and Present Levels of Performance

In addition to the descriptive information just given, an evaluation attached to Tammy's IEP mentioned that she would benefit from a vocational skills training program, that her low motivation is an ongoing problem, and that she needs orally presented instruction that is short, concrete, and step-by-step. Additional detail was also given about her academic levels.

Services

No services were specified beyond her enrollment in one study skills class. Her extreme need for speech and language therapy was ignored, as were her needs for vocational programming and for specific oral instruction. Based on Tammy's performance levels, a truly individualized program would have a large speech/language therapy component. Since low motivation is also a major concern, the IEP should address this directly and squarely. A source such as Thomas Lovitt's *Preventing School Dropouts* (1991) is invaluable for developing IEP components for high school students' motivation, social behaviors, attendance, compliance, self-concepts, and much more.

Goals and Objectives

The goals are perfectly vague and absolutely unmeasurable. Her one goal for study skills (see Figure 10) is a classic: "to improve basic and other life skills." Not only is that goal not measurable, but it is self-evident from the objectives and even more so from the "methods of evaluation" that no one ever, for even one second, intended to measure Tammy's progress!

Discussion

Tammy's IEP, like so many, deals only with academics. It denies FAPE in several ways. Neither speech therapy nor vocational training was offered even though both were needed. The excerpts from her IEP illustrate a fairly common practice of pretending to "individualize" by filling in blanks with a percentage. For example, for the consumer education component (see Figure 11) there are objectives of creating a budget with 75% accuracy and using ten banking and money management vocabulary words with 75% accuracy. One can only wonder whether the latter means 7 ½ words will be used correctly or all ten words will be used 3/4 correctly. Her math skills do not include multiplication or division or fractions or decimals. The skills she does have will be extended by preparing a budget, even though it need be only <u>75%</u> accurate.

The English objective (see Figure 9) requires Tammy to explain the cultural beliefs or values being reflected in a personal view with <u>75%</u> accuracy. This may be slightly difficult for a young woman who responds orally with only one or two words or by pointing. And one can only wonder how it was decided that Tammy was a "<u>75%</u> person." The odds are very high that all students with disabilities in these classes have identical IEPs except, perhaps, for the percentages. In addition to denying needed services, not being the least bit individualized, and having meaningless and unmeasurable goals and objectives, Tammy's IEP also illustrates the "no-no" of being nothing more than excerpts from an ongoing regular curriculum.

J.R.

J.R. is a student who has a speech impairment. Selected portions of his IEPs from third, fourth, and fifth grades are shown in Figure 12. They speak for themselves. When a service has not been effective, something needs to change! And decreasing the amount of the same service is not an appropriate response. These excerpts are strong evidence of the failure of the district's program to rise to the level of legally appropriate. The parents could well consider obtaining private therapy and requesting the district to pay. The parents would probably prevail if the district refused.

Figure 12
J.R.

Selected Portions of J.R.'s IEPs

3rd Grade

Annual Goal(s)	Date Signed		Person(s) Responsible for Implementation	Hours/Week	Evaluation Criteria
	Special Education Related Services				
J will say correct "r" sounds with 90% accuracy in conversation	Speech therapy			40 min. (2 or 3 15-min. sessions per week)	- Picture test for articulation - Teacher-made criterion test - Sample of conversation

I/we have participated in the development of the above program and approve of educational services as described _____

4th Grade

Annual Goal(s)	Date Signed		Person(s) Responsible for Implementation	Hours/Week	Evaluation Criteria (annual)
	Special Education Related Services				
J will say correct "r" sounds with 90% accuracy in conversation	Speech therapy			40 min.	- Picture test for articulation - Teacher-made criterion test - Sample of conversation

I/we have participated in the development of the above program and approve of educational services as described _____

5th Grade

Annual Goal(s)	Date Signed		Person(s) Responsible for Implementation	Hours/Week	Evaluation Criteria
	Special Education Related Services				
J will say correct "r" sounds with 90% accuracy in conversation	Speech therapy			30 min. (2 or 3 15-min. sessions per week)	- Picture test for articulation(annual) - Teacher-made criterion test - Sample of conversation - Classroom teacher's observation

I/we have participated in the development of the above program and approve of educational services as described _____

This IEP also reveals yet another misuse of percentages. An "r" sound said with 90% accuracy is an "r" sound misarticulated, is it not? Surely the intent was to say that J.R.'s "r" sounds would be articulated clearly 90% of the time. Even so, why 90%? Why not 100%?

Kevin

Kevin's IEP (see Figure 13) illustrates yet another abuse of percentages combined with questionable evaluation methods. Is it really believable that once per quarter a resource room teacher and/or assistant will determine whether Kevin has decreased his inappropriate remarks to other students 90% of the time? How would one do that if one were truly trying to do so? Would that be practical? Reducing inappropriate remarks is clearly a good thing to do, but just to attach a number to it does **not** make it measurable. Many goal writers seem to mistakenly believe that is all that is required, even though the number attached makes no sense, as here.

Figure 13
Kevin

I.E.P.

GOALS AND OBJECTIVES
(Primary Service Provider)

Status Key   C - Completed
D - Dropped
R - Revised
N - Parent Notified

Student's Name   Kevin   **Date** March 8, 1989

Present Level of Performance In Socialization skills and behavior are below average according to checklists filled out by parents and teachers

Annual Goal Statement Kevin will demonstrate improved socialization skills and behavior by 3/90

Short-Term Objectives	Criteria	Evaluation Method	Scheduled Evaluation	Position Responsible	Status	Date
Kevin will be able to:						
1) Improve attention during teacher-directed lesson	80% of the time	Teacher observation	Quarterly	ERC teacher & assistants		
2) Improve requested standard behaviors from one class to the next including: standing in line, walking, & following directions	85% of the time	Teacher observation	Ongoing	ERC teacher & assistants		
3) Decrease inappropriate remarks to other students	90% of the time	Teacher observation	Quarterly	ERC teacher & assistants		
4) React appropriately when adult gives corrections	90% of the time	Teacher observation	Weekly	ERC teacher & assistants		
5) Increase eye contact with adults and peers	85% of the time	Teacher observation	Weekly	ERC teacher & assistants		

Original - Teacher   Canary - Parent   Pink - Cumulative File   Goldenrod - District Rep.

Kevin's behaviors are reasonably well-targeted. However, social behaviors can sometimes be quite difficult to convert to appropriate IEP components. Sugai and Colvin's (1990) tips for writing goals and objectives for social behaviors are presented in Chapter Four. These would have been very helpful to the people writing Kevin's IEP.

Schools have become so accustomed to certain ways of writing IEPs that it would be helpful to sometimes stop and ask if a given component makes any sense. For example, what does it mean that Kevin will increase eye contact 85% of the time? Will this be checked once per week? How will that work? What data will the teacher actually collect? How? When? It is obvious that many IEPs like this one were never intended to be taken seriously, never intended to serve as an objective monitor for the efficacy of the services provided.

This IEP specifies no services. What will the district do to enable Kevin to improve attention, decrease his inappropriate remarks, and so on? Or is Kevin to "choose" these behavioral changes on his own? This kind of disconnectedness between PLOPs and goals and objectives is too common, as IEPs like this one focus only on what the student will do, not on what the district will provide.

Andy

Andy was a nonreader after three years in school. Then his parents independently found a private clinic that successfully taught Andy using the Lindamood Auditory Discrimination in Depth program. They went to hearing and won all their expenses, including transportation time as well as mileage and all tutoring costs. Additionally, they won all legal fees related to the hearing. The legal issue was whether the IEP (see Figure 14) provided FAPE to Andy.

The hearing officer pointed out, among many other and even more serious problems, that Andy's teacher had completed the IEP before the meeting. It is evident there was no parental input. The total reliance on the Woodcock-Johnson (W-J) test is apparent when one recognizes that each objective reflects a W-J subtest. Andy's district was shown at hearing to rely totally and solely on the W-J for identification of students as learning disabled, for determining present levels of performance, for establishing goals and objectives, and for evaluation of progress.

Figure 14
Andy

I.E.P.

GOALS AND OBJECTIVES
(Primary Service Provider)

Status Key   C - Completed
              D - Dropped
              R - Revised
              N - Parent Notified

Date   11-20-89

Student's Name   Andy

Present Level of Performance In   Reading Ability - 2.3   Achievement 1.0 (3-1) according to Woodcock-Johnson

Psycho-Educational Battery

Annual Goal Statement   Andy will make six mo. to 1 year gain in reading by Nov. 1990 as measured by Woodcock-Johnson

Psycho-Educational Battery

Short-Term Objectives	Criteria	Evaluation Method	Scheduled Evaluation	Position Responsible	Status	Date
Andy will know and say letter names	100%	Commercial	Semester	ERC	C	11-9C
Andy will know and say letter sounds	100%	Commercial	Semester	ERC	C	11-9C
Andy will read sight words on a 1.5 to 2.0 grade level	85%	Commercial	Semester	ERC	Continue	11-9C
Andy will read sentences and short stories on a 1.5 to 2.0 grade level	85%	Commercial	Semester	ERC	C	11-9C
Andy will answer literal comprehension questions	85%	Commercial	Semester	ERC	C	11-9C

Original - Teacher   Canary - Parent   Pink - Cumulative File   Goldenrod - District Rep.

These "objectives" are all projected to be completed in a year. They are not the "how far, by when" progress markers toward goals that objectives are expected to be. It is also unrealistic to believe the W-J (the "commercial" evaluation method) is actually going to be given each semester every year. Nor should it be.

Finally, a projected gain of six months to one year in the annual goal is totally inadequate to allow Andy to catch up.

Ryan

Ryan is Andy's older brother. His third and sixth grade IEPs are both presented (see Figures 15 and 16). The district wisely settled his case without going to hearing. They paid for his private tutoring, transportation, and legal expenses just as they were ordered to do with Andy. Ryan's third grade IEP (Figure 15) and Andy's IEP (Figure 14) were written almost four years apart. The minor differences are related to different levels on the W-J. Three years later, now in the sixth grade (Figure 16), Ryan was still reading at a third grade level, having gained only one year during three years, and fallen that much further behind.

Figure 15
Ryan

I.E.P.

GOALS AND OBJECTIVES
(Primary Service Provider)

Status Key   C - Completed
D - Dropped
R - Revised
N - Parent Notified

Student's Name   Ryan   **Date**   1-23-86

Present Level of Performance In   Reading Letter Identification - 4.3; Word Ident. - 1.9; Word Attack - 1.6; Word

Comprehension - 1.4; Passage Comprehension - 2.3; Total - 2.1, as measured by Woodcock Reading Mastery Test

Annual Goal Statement   Ryan will make 1 year's gain in reading by Jan., 1987 as measured by Woodcock-Johnson

Reading Test

Short-Term Objectives	Criteria	Evaluation Method	Scheduled Evaluation	Position Responsible	Status	Date
1. Ryan will read sight words on a 2.9 grade level	85%	Commercial	Semester	ERC	Complete	12-15-86
2. Ryan will use decoding skills for unknown words	85%	Commercial	Semester	ERC	Complete	12-15-86
3. Ryan will complete analogies on a 2nd-grade level	85%	Commercial	Semester	ERC	Complete	12-15-86
4. Ryan will read short stories on a 3rd-grade level	85%	Commercial	Semester	ERC	Complete	12-15-86
5. Ryan will answer literal and inferential comprehension questions	85%	Commercial	Semester	ERC	Complete	12-15-86

Original - Teacher   Canary - Parent   Pink - Cumulative File   Goldenrod - District Rep.

Figure 16
Ryan

I.E.P.

Status Key   C - Completed
              D - Dropped
              R - Revised
              N - Parent Notified

GOALS AND OBJECTIVES
(Primary Service Provider)

Student's Name   Ryan   **Date**   11-9-88

Present Level of Performance In   Reading achievement is 3.3 as measured by the Woodcock-Johnson

6th Grade

Annual Goal Statement   Ryan will make 6 months' to 1 year's gain in reading achievement by November, 1989 as

measured by Woodcock-Johnson Psycho-Educational Battery

Short-Term Objectives	Criteria	Evaluation Method	Scheduled Evaluation	Position Responsible	Status	Date
1. Ryan's progress in reading will be monitored in the regular classroom	passing grade	grades and teacher observation	monthly	regular classroom teacher and resource teacher		

Original - Teacher   Canary - Parent   Pink - Cumulative File   Goldenrod - District Rep.

The district's response was to do nothing, i.e., to "monitor" Ryan in the regular classroom. One has to wonder how, if at all, this sixth grade IEP meets the requirements for: (1) specification of special education and related services (delivered by qualified/certified special education personnel), and (2) measurable behavioral objectives. These "monitoring" or "consulting" IEPs are becoming more and more common as more children are educated full-time in regular classrooms. If the student no longer needs special education, perhaps his or her IDEA eligibility should be reevaluated. If a legitimate monitoring period is part of that determination one would expect the IEP to contain specific classroom modifications and very precise criteria and evaluation procedures. Too few "monitoring" or "consulting" IEPs contain these provisions.

All three of Andy and Ryan's IEPs reveal a total lack of individualization and a built-in "behindedness." They all project a totally inadequate annual gain of six months to a year. Worse yet, the actual reading programs provided the boys were as bad or worse than the IEPs! The district personnel obviously had **a** procedure for writing IEPs and that procedure did not in any way include looking at the individual student. Rather, only the test was considered.

A Summary of IEP Sins

The sins we've highlighted in these real IEPs (and see Figure 17) are common and they occur in varying degrees of "wrongness." A district's entire program for a child may be declared a denial of FAPE if sins in the IEP render it so. Among the worst of these are the failure to individualize (often revealed in computer generation and in misuse of percentages); failure to address all needs; failure to specify services adequately; and writing vague, meaningless, and unmeasurable PLOPs, objectives, and goals.

Figure 17

IEP SINS

I.   FAILURE TO INDIVIDUALIZE THE PROGRAM TO FIT THE STUDENT

II. FAILURE TO ADDRESS ALL THE STUDENT'S NEEDS

III. FAILURE TO SUFFICIENTLY DESCRIBE AND SPECIFY ALL NECESSARY SERVICES

IV. FAILURE TO WRITE CLEAR, OBJECTIVE, MEANINGFUL, AND REASONABLE PLOPS, OBJECTIVES, AND GOALS

Now, having looked at how not to write an IEP, we'll get on with doing it the right way in the next chapter.

Educationally Useful IEPs: Doing it a Better Way

A Better Way

In recognition of past widespread problems and inadequacies in IEPs, the U.S. Office of Education (Hehir, 1997) has placed new emphasis on several crucial aspects of IEPs. One aspect is an explicit and badly needed focus on the child's **unique needs** arising from the disability. Related to this is an emphasis on what needs must be met and services provided to enable the student to **access the general curriculum**, as appropriate. This, in turn, has led to the inclusion of a **regular educator** on the IEP team for any child who is or may be placed in a regular classroom. In response to the fact that half of learning disabled students have been receiving no accommodations in regular classrooms, new attention is directed to the required provision of those necessary **accommodations in regular classes**. Other minor changes, including special considerations for some students according to individual needs, were listed in Chapter Three and appear on our recommended IDEA "Non-Form" (see Figures 19a, b, and c later in this chapter).

The heart of better IEP development is a sequential, three-fold inquiry made by the IEP team: (1) What are this child's unique educational characteristics/needs that must be taken into account in a truly individualized education program? (2) What will the district do/provide in response to each of these characteristics/needs? (3) If the services are effective, what goals and objectives will the child reach? In other words, what accomplishments will indicate the services are on the right track?

These three inquiries are the major focus of the IEP meeting. Illustrative Non-Form IEPs and some examples of unique characteristics/needs, district responses/services, and goals and objectives that serve to evaluate the services will be presented in this chapter. But first, let's look at the IEP process itself.

Preparation for the IEP Meeting

The initial responsibility for setting the stage for a successful IEP meeting is on the district, and usually specifically on the special education teacher or case manager. Of all the IEP meetings a parent may attend, none is likely to be more crucial than the first. Parents need to be informed that their role in the IEP meeting is not the familiar one of a parent-teacher conference. In the latter, the teacher tells the parent about the child, and the parent perhaps asks an occasional question. Often parents have no reason to think the IEP meeting is going to be any different. It is up to the school personnel to make sure the parents' role is as full and equal participants in the IEP meeting.

In order to participate fully and effectively parents need to understand the kind of input from them that will be most helpful. The parents' invitation to the first IEP meeting (see Figure 18) could include a sample IEP that has been developed for a hypothetical child who has some characteristics/needs similar to those of their child. It is also useful to enclose a list of questions about their child's characteristics/needs and strengths, so the parents arrive at the meeting prepared to discuss them. Encourage the parents to consider carefully whether it would be beneficial to have the child present at the IEP meeting or some portion of the meeting. If the child will not be present at the entire meeting, display a large photo of him or her to help the IEP team stay focused on the task of creating a program individualized for that student. Ask the parents to be ready to share any concerns they have about their child's educational program.

Figure 18
Sample IEP Meeting Invitation

Dear Mr. and Mrs. Stein,

As you know, we recently determined that your daughter Abigail was eligible for an Individualized Education Program (IEP) to meet her special academic, social, behavioral, physical, or other needs. She is now legally entitled to: (1) special education, which is specially designed instruction to meet those unique needs; (2) related services such as transportation or physical therapy, which may be necessary to enable her to benefit from her special education; and (3) any necessary services, aids, modifications, or accommodations if and when she is in regular education classes, including support for the personnel working with her.

We need to have a meeting to plan Abigail's IEP. At this meeting, we will discuss her strengths, her unique characteristics and needs, the services appropriate to address these, and the ways we should judge how well the services are helping Abigail to make progress at school. You are a full and equal partner with the school personnel in deciding what will be included in Abigail's IEP. The enclosed sample IEP for a fictional child will give you an idea of what kinds of things an IEP might include. Please give some thought to these matters ahead of time, so we can exchange ideas at the meeting.

You are welcome to bring anyone you wish who is knowledgeable about your child to the meeting. Some parent groups (e.g., Learning Disabilities Association, Association for Retarded Citizens) have advocates available to attend IEP meetings with parents. You may choose to have Abigail present for all or part of the meeting. It is often useful for the student to participate, and she may feel more involved with and committed to her IEP objectives if she does so. If you decide Abigail won't be at the meeting, please consider bringing a picture of her to remind us all that the only purpose of the meeting is to plan an educational program just for her. Pam Brown, who helped evaluate Abigail, and Nancy Janes, her regular classroom teacher, will be at this first IEP meeting. The principal, Denise Smith, will attend the IEP meeting as the district representative, and I will be there as Abigail's special education teacher.

We have tentatively scheduled this meeting for Feb. 2 at 3:00 PM here at McAuliffe Elementary. If this is not convenient, please call and we will arrange another time. In addition to the sample IEP, I have enclosed a brochure explaining your legal rights. Please look it over. If you have any questions, we can discuss them at the meeting.

Sincerely,

Anita Hall

Anita Hall
Abigail's Special Education Teacher

The invitation should set a tone of mutual cooperation and problem solving. It can also explain, in understandable language, the child's legal **entitlement to services** and suggest that the parents may want to have someone accompany them to the IEP meeting. The IDEA anticipates the school district will fully, repeatedly, and meaningfully inform parents of all their rights. Much experience has shown that this does not usually happen. Many parents have little awareness of the types of individualized services to which their child may be entitled. It is solely and squarely the district's responsibility to inform the parents about these entitlements. The IDEA now mandates that a statement of parents' **procedural protections** be given to them upon each notification of an IEP meeting, as well as other times. Information about parents' rights, which could be used to generate such a statement, appears in Appendix D.

The school's preparation for the IEP meeting should include a review of the child's evaluation and his or her progress, as both will be discussed at the meeting. Teachers often feel a need to prepare at least a portion of the IEP prior to the meeting. At the first IEP meeting, especially, this might improperly convey to the parents that IEP meetings are one more "school tells parent" situation, rather than the desired message of full and equal partnership. The primary legal concern is with the parents' opportunity to participate. Therefore, the law does not prohibit any IEP participant from coming to the meeting with prepared notes. However, it is both illegal and counterproductive to draft the entire IEP and simply present it to the parents as a finished product.

All school personnel who participate regularly in the IEP process should review, at least annually, the IDEA regulations (see Appendix B) and Appendix C of IDEA (see Appendix C) which pertain to IEPs. Parents should also be informed of the existence of the regulations and Appendix C of IDEA, and given copies and the opportunity to become familiar with them if they wish.

The Setting

Above all else, the setting for the IEP meeting should be as physically comfortable and free of distractions as possible. Under no circumstances, ever, should the meeting be held in a classroom where the parents are required to sit in small chairs or at uncomfortably low tables. All required participants should plan to be present for the entire meeting. Make sure that any records, work samples, or instructional materials necessary for consultation are present and easy to reach. Allow no interruptions for unrelated messages or phone calls. However, it can be very useful to have a speaker phone available if, for example, the child's doctor or previous teacher or speech therapist, etc. needs to provide brief input but has no need to be present for the entire meeting.

Allot ample time for the meeting so no one feels rushed. At the same time, it is important to keep the session focused, on-task, and moving along. First IEP meetings often require an hour or so. Annual reviews can usually be shorter. Very difficult and complicated IEPs can take several hours or sessions, especially if communication and trust have broken down as is too often the case when a child's needs are very complex.

It may be helpful in many, if not all, meetings to have an easel and large sheets of paper for true group development of the IEP. Later, copy the actual IEP onto the proper form and send a copy to the parents. There is no requirement (and never was) that the parents be present when the official version of the IEP is finalized. The mandate is for the parents to have every opportunity for full and meaningful participation in the development of the substance of the IEP.

The question of tape recording may arise. It is wise to record all IEP meetings, except perhaps the most routine, unless the parents object. If the district keeps a tape, it becomes part of the student's education record. If the parents keep the tape, it is not an education record. Sometimes school personnel fear that the very process of recording may inhibit or change the flow of ideas. If this is true, repeated experience will quickly solve the problem. Experience also shows taping reduces the likelihood of inappropriate remarks or wrong information being offered.

Remind everyone that the "I" in IEP stands for individualized, that special education is defined as "... specially designed instruction to meet the child's unique education needs" (34 CFR 300.24 (a)(1)), and that the IEP will address the child's unique needs or characteristics as well as all the specially designed instruction, services, modifications, and accommodations these needs or characteristics necessitate. At this stage, there is a strong temptation for some who have written old-style IEPs in the past to revert to thinking about a preexisting, ongoing program (such as the resource room reading program) and be tempted to write goals and objectives from or for that program. Avoid that temptation at all costs! The meeting is about the individual child, not about the resource teacher's favorite reading program.

Now, pull comfortable chairs up to the round oak table, serve the relaxing herbal tea, turn on the tape recorder, and put the newsprint tablet on the easel. It's time to develop the IEP.

The Non-Form

No more structured or detailed form than our recommended IEP Non-Form (see Figures 19a, b, and c) should be allowed in the meeting. Blank pages are even better. Too often the forms commonly used interfere with creative, flexible individualization. The form is interfering unduly whenever one has to ask, "Where on the form do I put that?" Whatever IEP form is used, if any, must facilitate the process, not interfere with it. The first page of the Non-Form, largely comprised of 1998 requirements, is self-explanatory. The second page is the heart of the IEP—the three-part sequence from needs to services to goals. The last page contains additional 1998 requirements and transition components.

Form need not and should not prevail over substance. For example, a present level of performance (PLOP) can logically appear in either the first or the third column of Figure 19b, depending upon preference and ease. For now, stop a moment and get to know the Non-Form. It can become a best friend.

Also remember that the IDEA requires that the means for evaluating progress toward goals be included. This is usually best done explicitly in the behavioral objectives. However, if the behavioral objectives do not include them, they would have to be added. Also, the IEP must include the amount, the location, the beginning date, and duration of related services to be provided.

Figure 19a

Non-Form
Individualized Education Program

Student's Name _____ Grade _____ Primary Contact Person/Case Manager _____

Date of Birth _____ Date of IEP Meeting _____

Copies of this IEP will circulate among staff members who are working with this student. Please observe the Federal and state laws that protect the student's right to confidentiality of education records. Do NOT share with unauthorized persons, and do NOT include sensitive information such as disability category or IQ.

Participants

Signature	Position

Special Factors to Consider

For all students, consider:
- ☐ Strengths of the student
- ☐ Concerns of the parent(s)
- ☐ Need for assistive technology

If behavior impedes learning of the student or others, consider:
- ☐ Strategies, including positive behavioral interventions
- ☐ Supports to address behavior

If the student has limited English proficiency, consider:
- ☐ Language needs as they relate to the student's IEP

If the student is blind or visually impaired, consider:
- ☐ Instruction in the use of Braille (unless the IEP team decides instruction in Braille is inappropriate)

Consider communication needs (language & communication needs for students with hearing impairments), including:
- ☐ Opportunities for direct communication with peers and professionals in the student's language and communication mode
- ☐ Opportunities for direct instruction in the student's language and communication mode

Figure 19b

Unique Educational Needs, Characteristics, and Present Levels of Performance (PLOPs) *(including how the disability affects the student's ability to progress in the general curriculum)*	Special Education, Related Services, Supplemental Aids & Services, Assistive Technology, Program Modifications, Support for Personnel *(including frequency, duration, & location)*	Measurable Annual Goals & Short-Term Objectives or Benchmarks • To enable the student to participate in the general curriculum • To meet other needs resulting from the disability *(including how progress toward goals will be measured)*

Figure 19c

Transition Planning

_____(The student)_____ has reached age 14, and _____(his or her)_____ :
(a) goals for life after high school include _____

(b) course of study is linked to student transition goals by _____

_____(The student)_____ has reached age 16, and:
(a) the following activities are needed to promote transition to post-high school life

• Instruction _____

• Related services _____

• Community experiences _____

• Development of employment and other adult living objectives _____

• Acquisition of daily living skills & functional vocational evaluation _____

(b) _____(The student)_____ does not need one or more of the activies listed above because _____

_____(The student)_____ will reach the age of majority under state law on _(date)_.
(He or she) has received notice (at least a year in advance) of all rights under the IDEA that will transfer to _(him or her)_ at that time.

_____
Student's Signature

Progress Reports

The parents will receive regular reports about _____(the student's)_____
(a) progress toward achieving annual goals

(b) and the extent to which that progress is sufficient to enable achievement of goals by the end of the year

Progress reports will take the form of _____

and the parents will receive them _____ times/year (which is at least as often as parents of children who are not on IEPs receive progress reports).
Reports will include **specific** information about progress on each IEP goal.

Participation With Nondisabled Students

Explanation of the extent to which _____(the student)_____ will **not** participate with nondisabled children in (a) regular classes _____

(b) special education services _____

Participation in State- and District-Wide Assessments

(The student) needs the following modifications in the administration of state- or district-wide assessments _____

The IEP team has decided that _(the student)_ will **not** participate in any state- or district-wide assessments
(a) because _____

(b) _(The student)_ will instead be assessed by _____

• _Better IEPs_ •

Developing the IEP

"Repetition is the mother of learning," says a Russian adage, so accordingly we re-peat here that the heart of effective IEP development is the three-fold inquiry made by the IEP team: (1) What are this child's unique educational charac-teristics/needs that must be taken into account in a truly individualized education program? (2) What will the district do/provide in response to each of these charac-teristics/needs? (3) If the services are effective, what goals and objectives will the child reach? In other words, what student accomplishments will indicate the serv-ices are on the right track?

Before beginning, make sure the legally required individuals are present, espe-cially those who know the child well. Remember that someone who has expertise in the instructional implications of evaluation must be there, as well as a qualified district representative who can allocate district resources and guarantee that no administrative veto of the IEP team decisions will occur. After the brief greetings and amenities described previously, IEP development is ready to begin.

The Student's Unique Characteristics/Needs/ Present Levels of Performance (PLOPs)

The IEP team must determine the student's unique characteristics/needs to which special services must be directed. One helpful way to learn to think in terms of these essential characteristics is to imagine that you are describing the child to a volunteer who has never met the child and is going to take him or her to an out-door education camp for a week. What would the volunteer need to know about **this** child that wouldn't be predicted from age or sex alone? The IEP is required to address only the portions or aspects of the child's education that need to be in-dividualized. The child should be visible in the IEP. Too many IEPs reveal only the academic program available in the resource room and show nothing whatso-ever about the child. The primary focus of the IEP will be the specification of serv-ices. This initial step is to determine what it is about this child that necessitates the services. Every **need** of the child must be addressed by a **service** (e.g., the child needs a quiet, highly structured work space) or by a **goal and a service** (if the service is instructional).

When a legal dispute arises about a child's program, frequently one of the central issues is whether the services provided addressed all the child's special needs—those special needs that must be specified in this first step of IEP development. It is difficult to imagine how one could either attack or defend the services offered to meet a child's unique needs unless those needs had been specified. In addition to the real-world knowledge the IEP team members have about the student's characteristics/needs, it may be helpful to consult any current evaluations of the child. This is particularly important for the first IEP which immediately follows the evaluation which found the child to be an IDEA eligible student with a disability. In the past, many evaluations failed to address a child's special needs. The law now requires that all evaluations include information which leads directly to educational planning. Parents must be prepared to insist that such evaluations replace the old-style assessment focused solely on eligibility. Schools must recognize that evaluation personnel may need additional support and training to meet this new and highly important change in the legal requirements for assessment.

Describing the Student's Needs

Judges and hearing officers have described learning disabled students' needs in these words taken verbatim from cases:

> The student needs reteaching and repetition, small classes, flexible programming, computer access and training (SEA Conn., *Farmington Bd. of Ed.*, 24 IDELR 1067 (1996)); this student needs a highly structured environment, small campus, small classes, frequent teacher feedback, clear commands, individualized attention, and consistent behavior management (*Capistrano Unified S.D. v. Wartenberg*, 59 F.3d 884 (9th Cir., 1995)); this student needs daily multisensory reading, spelling, and writing, needs never to hear "if only he worked harder," and he needs to be with other dyslexics (*Evans v. Bd. of Rhinebeck Central S.D.*, 930 F. Supp. 83 (S.D.N.Y., 1996)); he needs full-time learning support and extended school year, as well as help with organization and attention (SEA Pa., *Western Wayne S.D.*, 25 IDELR 867 (1997)).

Smith and Strick (1997) have listed these ten needs common to many students who have learning disabilities: (1) manageable class size (i.e., below 25); (2) limited distractions; (3) an active, guiding teacher who monitors, keeps the students on task, models respect, and offers encouragement; (4) a noncompetitive atmosphere; (5) an orderly, structured, on-task approach to learning; (6) a focus on basic skills; (7) instructional flexibility, including peer tutors, study partners, etc.; (8) clear expectations for achievement; (9) effective, data-based monitoring of pupil performance; and (10) ample positive feedback. At least some of these, as they fit the individual student, should appear on the IEPs of many learning disabled students.

Too often schools have tended to think of needs only in terms of, "she needs 45 minutes per day in the resource room," for example. But the examples just given, from cases and a textbook, illustrate a style of thinking about needs that leads directly to educational services.

Characteristics/needs of the child will often "cluster." The team may well decide in the next step that one service will address more than one characteristic/need. However, at this point it is important to just brainstorm and list all the unique characteristics that require individualized attention. Sometimes the natural flow seems to work across the second page (Figure 19b) of the IEP Non-Form, i.e., when a characteristic/need has been identified to next move to what service or accommodation will address it and then, when the service is instructional, on to the goals for that service. Other times it may feel better to list all the characteristics, then move to services, and then to goals. Either way or a combination of both is perfectly okay.

Present Levels of Performance

The law requires that the student's present level of performance (PLOP) be indicated in a readily understandable way that is sufficiently precise for progress to be measured. Sometimes the PLOP is contained in the characteristic itself (e.g., has **no** friends, **always** plays alone at recess, **never** volunteers in class, was absent **80 of 175** days, is tardy to class **at least once daily**). Other times it can best be presented as the beginning point in a sequence of PLOP → objectives → goal. For example, suppose the characteristic is slow, inaccurate decoding, and the present level of performance is 15-20 words per minute (WPM) with three to eight errors in second grade material. The first objective might be 25-35 WPM/0-2 errors, the second objective 50 WPM/0-2 errors, and the goal 80 WPM/0-2 errors in second grade material.

Thus PLOP is either an elaboration of the characteristic/need or the chronological beginning point in the succession of PLOP → objectives → goal. The PLOP is now, the objectives are next, and the goal is where the student is headed. Figure 20 illustrates the PLOP as a quantified characteristic, and Figure 21 shows the PLOP as a beginning point for the goal.

Figure 20
Illustrative Sequence: PLOP as a Measurable Characteristic

Characteristics/Needs/PLOPs	Service	Goal/Objectives
1. Terri's handwriting is very slow, awkward, and poor. PLOP: 10 letters copied per minute with 2-4 illegible.	1. Two 2-minute probes daily with number of legible letters copied per minute graphed and rewarded by a point system or by self-charting.	1. Annual goal: copy/generate 40 letters per minute with 40 legible. Obj.1: 20 letters with <2 illegible, by Dec 1.

Figure 21
Illustrative Sequence: PLOP as Part of PLOP → Objectives → Goal

Characteristics/Needs	Service	PLOP/Objectives/Goal
1. Terri's handwriting is very slow, awkward, and poor.	1. Two 2-minute probes daily with number of legible letters copied per minute graphed and rewarded by a point system or by self-charting.	PLOP: 10 letters copied per minute with 2-4 illegible. Goal: Copy/generate 40 letters per minute with 40 legible. Obj.1: 20 letters with <2 illegible, by Dec 1.

Sometimes a present level of performance is best described by a work sample, which can be attached to the IEP. A picture can speak very loudly, as in the handwriting sample shown in Figure 22. Notice how the quality of the content of the writing can be seen in spite of the near illegibility. Transcripts or even tapes of oral reading of a few sentences can also be very useful.

Figure 22
Work Sample as a PLOP

The relationship of the PLOP to the goal must be clear. One way to write IEPs, which makes this connection clearly, is to move from present level of performance to the needed service, and then to the goal and objectives. For example, an IEP writing sequence for a child who has a reading disability might be as follows:

1. **Present level of performance:** Reads first grade material at 20-30 words per minute with 5-10 errors, guesses at all unknown words.

2. **Service to be provided:** One-to-one tutoring in highly structured reading program; five sessions weekly; 45 minutes each; provided in private, quiet area of resource room.

3. **Annual goal:** Will read third grade material at 80-100 words per minute with 0-2 errors.

    a. **Objective #1:** By December 15 will read second grade material at 40-60 words per minute with 0-5 errors.

    b. **Objective #2:** By March 15 will read third grade material at 50 words per minute with 0-4 errors.

The same relationship between present level of performance and the goal can be seen in a nonacademic area:

1. **Present level of performance:** Several times (five to ten) daily student draws or talks inappropriately about bodily functions.

2. **Service provided:** Behavioral contingency plan with student-selected reward and response cost.

3. **Annual goal:** No inappropriate talk or drawings about bodily functions.

    a. **Objective #1:** By February 1, fewer than 2 such inappropriate drawings or vocalizations per week.

    b. **Objective #2:** By April 15 maintain fewer than 2 such inappropriate drawings or vocalizations per month.

Examples of characteristics (not all from the same student) in both academic and social-emotional-behavioral areas follow. Remember that for each, the next inquiry will be, "What will the district do about this?" And then the last inquiry will be, "How will we know if that service is effective?"

These examples of unique characteristics/needs in academic areas reveal how some do, and some don't, need further refinement to become a measurable PLOP:

1. Handwriting slow, labored, "drawn," and nearly illegible due to improper size and spacing of letters and words. (PLOP: Writes legibly at a rate of x letters per minute.)

2. Lacks understanding of place value and regrouping in both addition and subtraction. (No PLOP needed, as a zero rate can be assumed.)

3. Attributes literal, concrete meaning to everything he hears and reads. (No PLOP needed.)

4. Understands spoken language, decodes words accurately but does not comprehend material read independently, oral reading reveals severe lack of expression and no attention to punctuation. (PLOP: Comprehension score of 3.1

grade equivalent on the XYZ test; decoding approximately 5th-6th grade level.)

5. Works very slowly, becomes upset if she makes a mistake, quits, and refuses to continue if paper is "messy." (No PLOP needed, or could elect to state an approximate rate of occurrence, e.g., twice daily.)

6. Answers before thinking, in both oral and written work; work is impulsive; many "careless" errors. (No PLOP needed, or could elect to state approximate rate of occurrence, e.g., 10-15 times daily.)

7. Gets arithmetic problems "messed up" and copies them incorrectly off board and out of book. Lines up problems incorrectly and also lines up answers wrong in multiplication and division. (PLOP: More than half of his arithmetic problems are wrong due to these errors.)

Some examples of unique characteristics/needs in social-emotional-behavioral areas would be:

1. Shy, no friends, never volunteers in class, never initiates social contact with other children.

2. Bully, doesn't know how to play with other children.

3. Overreacts and has temper outbursts, is noncompliant, pouts and whines, is sullen and negative when suggestions are made.

4. Short attention span, easily distracted by sounds.

Social behaviors such as these can be converted into IEP components, as shown by Sugai and Colvin (1990), in a series of steps. They recommend more than is required to be included in the IEP, but the steps are helpful:

- Problem Behavior—Behavior displayed by student that is observed and determined to be problematic (e.g., student does not follow adult directions the first time).

- Problem Context—Setting(s) or condition(s) in which behavior is most problematic (e.g., when in 45-minute, large group math or reading lessons).

- Desired Behavior—Replacement behavior selected for the problem behavior (e.g., student follows adult directions within five seconds without comment or inappropriate facial expression).

- Current Level of Functioning—How often or long occurrences of the problem and replacement behavior are exhibited (e.g., student follows teacher directions within five seconds in 45% of the opportunities).

- Desired Level of Functioning—How often or long occurrences of the problem and replacement behavior are desired (e.g., student follows teacher directions within five seconds in 90% of the opportunities for five consecutive days).

- Intervention Strategies—The names of possible strategies for achieving the desired level of functioning (e.g., behavioral contract, token economy, self-recording sheet, peer tutor).

- Evaluation Measurement—Type of measurement strategy for assessing student progress and intervention effectiveness (e.g., frequency counts of following and not following teacher directions).

- Evaluation Schedule—Schedule for how often measurements should be conducted (e.g., frequency counts will be daily for 45 minutes during math and reading groups).

Those elements mandated to be on the IEP are shown on T's fictitious partial IEP (see Figure 23), which uses the Sugai and Colvin procedure. This IEP also illustrates how the PLOP may be either part of the characteristic/need or the beginning point in the present level of performance ➔ objectives ➔ goal sequence. (Other such examples appear in the sample IEPs later in this chapter. Also at the end of the chapter, we will discuss a newly mandated IEP component, functional assessment and behavioral intervention plans.)

Figure 23
T's IEP (Partial)

Unique Educational Needs, Characteristics, and Present Levels of Performance (PLOPs) *(including how the disability affects the student's ability to progress in the general curriculum)*	Special Education, Related Services, Supplemental Aids & Services, Assistive Technology, Program Modifications, Support for Personnel *(including frequency, duration, & location)*	Measurable Annual Goals & Short-Term Objectives or Benchmarks • To enable student to participate in the general curriculum • To meet other needs resulting from the disability *(including how progress toward goals will be measured)*
T. does not follow adult directions the first time.	Token economy; behavioral contract. Services begin 1/21/98 and continue for 2 months, in all classrooms. Aides and regular teachers will receive one-hour training and handouts on the classroom use of a token economy (by 12/5/97).	Goal: Follow appropriate adult directions within 5 seconds without negative comment or facial expression. Obj. 1: Will do so in 75% of the opportunities for 3 consecutive days by 2/15. Obj. 2: Will do so in 90% of the opportunities for 5 consecutive days by 3/15. *(PLOP could also be in this column.)*

PLOP: Follows adult directions within 5 seconds about 45% of the time.

Special Education and Related Services

The second essential inquiry in the IEP process asks, "What will the district do in response to the child's needs?" These "District Do's" include special education, related services, regular class modifications, personnel support, and other creative, flexible, innovative, and often inexpensive ways to meet needs. This listing of services becomes the "special education and related services" which the law requires to be specified on the IEP. Too often this is omitted or simply perverted into a mere placement check mark or a percentage of time in special education (which now must be justified, as seen in Figure 19c). The amount of related services, such as speech therapy or physical therapy, must be shown, along with the beginning date for the service, the location, and the anticipated duration of the service.

Services to Allow Access to the General Curriculum

As pointed out at the beginning of this chapter, one of the new emphases of the IDEA is on addressing student needs and providing services related to allowing the student to access the general curriculum. We must make a critical distinction between services which allow the student to **access the curriculum** (such as following teacher directions, reading at grade level, etc.) versus **incorporating the general curriculum itself** into the IEP, which is not appropriate (see Figure 9 in Chapter Three for a classic example of this error). Special education services are necessary to allow some students to progress in the general curriculum. It is these special services, **not** the general curriculum, that are to be in the IEP.

The question for the IEP team to ask is: "What does the student need in order to access and progress in the general curriculum?" The answer might include: intensive, effective remedial reading services, supplemented initially by texts on tape; a peer tutor; oral reports rather than written reports; etc. These are special services, supports, and accommodations that must be included in the IEP. The IEP must address special education and any needed changes in regular education, not the regular education curriculum itself. All persons concerned must understand this point so that IEPs don't become mere restatements of the regular education curriculum.

Methodology

One of the interesting issues about services is the question of whether methodology need be specified. If, for example, the service is remedial reading, must the method be spelled out? In general, the answer is no. In 1977 the original proposed IDEA regulations would have mandated the inclusion of methodology and instructional materials in IEPs. However, when the rules became final that proposed require-ment had been dropped. In the meantime, some states and districts had moved quickly and already developed forms that included methods and materials. It is not unusual to find those forms still in use.

Congress' present (1997) intention regarding methodology in the IEP is:

> … that while teaching and related services methodologies or approaches are an ap-propriate topic for discussion and consideration by the IEP team during IEP devel-opment or annual review, they are not expected to be written into the IEP. Furthermore, the Committee does not intend that changing particular methods or approaches necessitates an additional meeting of the IEP team. Specific day to day adjustments in instructional methods and approaches that are made by either a regular or special education teacher to assist a disabled child to achieve his or her annual goals would not normally require action by the child's IEP team. However, if changes are contemplated in the child's measurable annual goals, benchmarks, or short-term objectives, or in any of the services or program modifications, or other components described in the child's IEP, the LEA must ensure that the child's IEP team is reconvened in a timely manner to address those changes (H. Rep. No. 105-95 (1997, pp. 105-195)).

Methodology becomes a source of conflict when parents are convinced their child will receive benefit from a particular method and will not benefit from the method the district wants to use. The most frequently sought methods are a particular method of communication for children who are deaf, a highly structured applied behavioral analysis (e.g., ABA or Lovaas) method of teaching children who have autism, and/or intensive, systematic, phonics-based reading programs for children who are dyslexic or otherwise learning disabled. Almost all case law agrees that schools may usually select the method. However, in a few cases parents have been able to show that a particular method is necessary to allow the IEP to be "reason-ably calculated" to allow benefit. Most often the successful cases involve children who have autism. A few cases have been won when the judge understood that a dyslexic student required an intensive phonics program (e.g., *Susquenita S.D. v. Raelee S.*, 25 IDELR 120 (M.D. PA., 1996), aff'd 96 F.3d 78 (3rd Cir., 1997); *Evans v. Bd. of Ed. of Rhinebeck Central S.D.*, 930 F.Supp. 83 (S.D.N.Y., 1996); *Hawaii Dept. of Education v. Tara H.*, Civ. No 86-1161 (D.HI., 1987)). It is ex-tremely important to note, as no court has yet done, that when the U.S. Supreme Court said methodology should be left to the state (i.e., hearing officers and schools), it said so in the context of its questionable belief that schools have and employ expertise in all relevant, effective methods (*Board of Ed. v. Rowley*, 102 S.Ct. 3034 (1982)). This, of course, is not always the case.

Inservice Training for Staff

A common and interesting question related to these "District Do" services relates to inservice training for teachers. Suppose, for example, Rob has Tourette Syndrome and needs teachers who are knowledgeable about how his symptoms are affected by stress. The agreed upon service to be provided by the district is inservice training by the local physician for all the school staff. Does that "District Do" belong on Rob's IEP? Absolutely! The IDEA now names **personnel support** as a mandated service when it is needed. Although delivered indirectly, it is a service to meet Rob's unique need. One concern is that such a service doesn't lend itself directly to a goal formulated in terms of Rob's behavior. This concern is easily addressed by looking to what is hoped to occur in Rob's behavior as a result of having informed, empathic teachers who assist him in avoiding unnecessary stress. One obvious answer is improved academic performance. Other outcomes (goals) could be a direct decrease in frequency and severity of his symptoms and an increase in attendance.

Modifications in the Regular Classroom

For many years some districts resisted including on IEPs the needed modifications in the regular classroom. However, it is well-settled law that these must be included. A checklist of types of modifications (e.g., in grading, discipline, assignments, texts, tests, etc.) can be helpful to ensure all necessary modifications are addressed (see Figures 24a and b).

Figure 24a
Classroom Modifications Checklist

To be part of _____ 's IEP

Date _____

_____ (Initial by Participant)
_____ (Initial by Participant)
_____ (Initial by Participant)
_____ (Initial by Participant)

Directions: Write "all" if a modification is required in **all** classes where applicable. If it is needed only in a particular class, specify accordingly.

Modifications Related to INPUT of Information

Teacher Talk

_____ Directions restated; short, clear sequence of steps
_____ Seating near teacher; near chalkboard
_____ Slow, careful speech
_____ Simple vocabulary; check for student comprehension; use synonyms
_____ Allow student to tape class
_____ Tape particularly important information, directions for student
_____ Interpreter
_____ Other _____
_____ Other _____

Texts; Handouts

_____ Different text at student's reading level
_____ Provide highlighted texts; teach student to highlight
_____ Provide second copy of texts for student to keep at home
_____ Issue clear, readable mimeos, dittos, etc.
_____ Highlight worksheets and handouts
_____ Provide reader
_____ Provide tapes of text
_____ Other _____
_____ Other _____

Tests

_____ Administered orally by aide, teacher, peer tutor
_____ Untimed
_____ Other _____

Figure 24b

Modifications Related to OUTPUT of Information

Tests

_____ Taped responses instead of written
_____ Shortened
_____ Single word or phrase answers rather than complete sentences
_____ Objective rather than essay
_____ Other _____

Assignments

_____ Shortened with full credit _____ partial credit _____
_____ Taped rather than written
_____ Manuscript rather than cursive
_____ Demonstrations, drawings, models, etc. rather than writing
_____ Additional time for work in class _____ out of class _____
_____ Peer editing
_____ Other _____
_____ Other _____

Aids

_____ Calculator on assignments _____ on tests _____
_____ Franklin speller on assignments _____ on tests _____
_____ Advance info. on material to be recited in class or on questions
                          to be asked by teacher
_____ Special paper, overlays, etc. (Describe) _____
                          _____

Grades

_____ Pass/fail with credit toward regular diploma
_____ Pass/fall with no credit toward regular diploma
_____ Based on effort and so indicated on transcript _____
                          not so indicated _____
_____ Based on shortened assignments and reduced amount of
                          work but held to same quality standard as other students
_____ Other (Describe Fully) _____
                          _____
                          _____
                          _____

This form may be made part of the IEP by participants initialling above and attaching to the IEP.

Goals and Objectives

The last step, after a characteristic(s)/need(s)/PLOP(s) and the appropriate services to meet it or them have been specified, is to write an annual goal and two or three benchmarks or objectives. Writing goals and objectives begins with asking, "If the service we're providing is effective, what will we see in the student's behavior that tells us so?" The purpose of the mandated goals and objectives is to evaluate the service. One needs to know when or if it is necessary to change the service being provided. As long as one is on track and the child is making reasonable progress one just keeps going. That's why the objectives used for tracking are to be statements of **how far** the student will progress toward the annual goal (12-month objective) **by when**. Now that progress reporting must be done at least as frequently for students on IEPs as for those not on IEPs, it might be efficient to write an objective for each reporting period.

Sometimes one goal can evaluate a cluster of several services. For example, think of a secondary student who has a severe learning disability affecting his written expression. He might need several services, including keyboarding instruction, tutoring in writing, modifications in test taking and length of written assignments, substitution of oral presentations for some term papers, and modified grading. The entire service cluster could be reasonably evaluated in terms of the student's improved rates of successful course completion and attendance. Other goals could also be appropriate. The point is just as characteristics or needs often cluster to require one service, so services sometimes cluster and can be assessed by a common, single goal.

One of the common and major problems with goals and objectives is that they are not taken seriously by their writers, who have no intention of actually checking whether the student has reached them or not. It is as if they never understood the most basic tenet of the IEP—that one is going to try the listed services and **see if they work** for that student. The goals and objectives are to be **real**. They are not just legal requirements to be completed and filed. They are to be used to evaluate program effectiveness. Figure 25 illustrates the contrast.

Figure 25
Examples of Annual Goals

NOT Real Goals	Real Goals
Joe will have a better attitude toward school 80% of the time.	Joe will have no more than 5 unexcused absences/tardies this year.
Sara will make wise choices in her use of leisure time.	Sara will participate weekly in a supervised extracurricular activity.
Max will be 75% successful in the mainstream.	Max will maintain a C+ average in his regular classes.
Beth will show an appropriate level of upper body strength.	Beth will pass upper body strength items on the ABC fitness test.

Goals are measurable statements of what one believes the student can do in a year if the service provided is effective. Therefore it is only logical to look at where one is starting (PLOP), where one will be in a bit (objective), and where one is headed in a year (goal). The following examples illustrate this sequence.

Anne

PLOP:	Anne averages 10 unexcused absences/tardies per month.
Objective #1:	By Feb. 1 she will have fewer than 5 unexcused absences/tardies per month.
Objective #2:	By April 2 she will have fewer than 2 unexcused absences/tardies per month.
Goal:	From April through June 1 she will average fewer than 1/2 unexcused absence/tardy per month.

Toby

PLOP:	Toby submits fewer than half his homework assignments.
Objective #1:	By Nov. 15 he will have submitted 75% of all homework assignments.
Objective #2:	By Jan. 15 he will have submitted 85% of all homework assignments.
Goal:	By the end of the year he will regularly submit all assigned homework on time.

Jill

PLOP: Jill orally reads 6th grade material at a rate of 50-75 words per minute and correctly answers 30-40% of factual comprehension questions asked orally.

Objective #1: By Dec. 1 Jill will read 6th grade material orally at 75-100 words per minute with 0-2 errors and correctly answer 60% of factual comprehension questions.

Objective #2: By March 1 Jill will read 6th grade material orally at 100-125 words per minute with 0-2 errors and correctly answer more than 70% of factual questions.

Goal: By June 15 Jill will orally read 7th grade material at 75-100 words per minute with 0-2 errors and correctly answer 90-100% of factual questions.

The usefulness of annual goals and objectives in evaluating the services provided is, in large part, a function of how well those goals and objectives are written. Although we've provided many examples, a more detailed description of developing useful goals and objectives is beyond the scope of this book. However, the reader can find detailed discussions in *The Essentials of Teaching* (Bateman, 1992) and in the classic how-to *Preparing Instructional Objectives* (Mager, 1997).

Developing the Transition Component of the IEP

The transition component of the IEP is just that, one portion of the student's regular IEP. It is not a parallel document, a separate entity, or a "transition IEP." All the IEP development requirements and procedures discussed previously may apply to the transition component. The legal significance of transition being but one aspect of the IEP process is substantial. A student is entitled only to those transition services which, for that student, are either special education or related services necessary to enable the student to benefit from special education. The period of "benefit" to be considered has arguably been lengthened beyond school and into adult life, but the substantive entitlement is still only to special education and related services, not to those **plus** transition services.

We are all relatively new at incorporating transition services into the IEP and into the broader world. Few rulings are yet available to assist in understanding the requirements. However, transition activities which must be addressed, unless the

IEP team finds one or more unnecessary, are: (1) instruction; (2) related services; (3) community experiences; (4) the development of objectives related to employment; and (5) other post-school adult living activities.

One way to approach student needs is to envision a typical weekday and a typical weekend after secondary school. Is the student still living in his or her parents' home? Has she gotten an apartment? Does he know how to find apartment ads in the classifieds? How to respond to an ad? How to locate the address? What about social contacts? Is she attending any sort of post-secondary schooling? This kind of questioning will help the team focus on the individual student's situation and needs.

The exact process the IEP team undertakes in looking into and planning for a student's post-school future will differ from student to student, as it should. The essential elements which should not vary include student and family participation and the willingness of the IEP team to address all the areas of need: intensive and effective basic skills instruction (not just exposure and not just repetitive practice), explicit survival skills, graduation requirements, and transition.

One logical beginning point for the transition component itself is with the team reaching agreement about the individual student's needs with regard to the mandated areas: (1) instruction; (2) related services; (3) community experiences; (4) employment; and (5) other post-school adult living objectives. If the team deems it inappropriate to address an area, presumably because the student presents no unique needs, the IEP must include the basis for that determination (see Figure 19c). The student's needs, taking into account his or her interests and preferences, can be explored prior to the meeting, and substantial input should also be sought from the parents. Questionnaires are an appropriate way to begin the student and parental input process.

Self-advocacy is one of the most important transition skills for many students who have disabilities. The student's presentation of his or her needs at the IEP meeting may itself provide one opportunity to assess and discuss self-advocacy skills. Another concern for some students with learning disabilities is passing the examinations required to obtain a driver's license. One can use the same basic three-step inquiry process used in the rest of the IEP for the student's needs for self-advocacy and obtaining a driver's license. Figure 26 illustrates the inclusion of these on Jim's IEP.

Figure 26
Jim's IEP: Transition Components

Figure 26
Jim's IEP: Transition Components

Unique Educational Needs, Characteristics, and Present Levels of Performance (PLOPs)	Special Education, Related Services, Supplemental Aids & Services, Assistive Technology, Program Modifications, Support for Personnel, and Agency Linkages and Responsibilities (L&R)	Measurable Annual Goals & Short-Term Objectives or Benchmarks
(including how the disability affects the student's ability to progress in the general curriculum)	*(including frequency, duration, & location)*	• To enable student to participate in the general curriculum • To meet other needs resulting from the disability *(including how progress toward goals will be measured)*
Instruction 1. Self-advocacy PLOP: Jim is unaware of his legal rights under §504 & ADA, and he is unable to request appropriate accommodations he would need in given situations, such as a large lecture class.	1. Small group instruction from Special Ed teacher in relevant rights & procedures under §504, ADA, & IDEA. Role playing in describing needed accommodations to "employers" and "professors." Services to begin Tuesday, Sept. 15; two 30-minute sessions weekly until goals are met. (L&R) Protection & Advocacy will assist teacher and provide materials at no cost. (Verified by phone - M. Adams)	1. Goal: Appropriately explain to a potential employer, professor, or other representative of the post-school world what accommodations are needed and, if necessary, the basis for the request. Objectives: 1. By Dec. 15, Jim will pass (75%) of a 25-item objective test over basic rights and procedures under §504 & ADA. 2. By March 1, given 5 hypothetical situations of common denial of rights under §504 or ADA, he will correctly explain possible actions and defend choice of actions to be taken.
Community 2. Driver's License PLOP: Jim has been driving for a year on a learner's permit and is concerned that he cannot pass the written test required for his license, although he is confident of all his driving and related skills except map reading.	2. Within two weeks, the driver training instructor will inform Jim about accommodations available in the state, if any, for licensing persons with reading disabilities. Then she and Jim will develop a plan to follow through and that plan will be added to this IEP no later than Oct. 10. Instruction in appropriately obtaining assistance in: (a) route highlighting, and (b) map drawing will be incorporated into self-advocacy practice above. (L&R) DMV will assist instructor and will provide information on test accommodations. (Verified by phone - C. Thomas)	2. Goal: Jim will be a competent, licensed driver in this state before June 15 and will be able to obtain and follow highlighted maps and line maps. Objectives: 1. By Dec. 1, Jim will be able to describe correctly 8 of 10 times how he would get from A to B following a highlighted map, and he will 8 of 10 times succeed in getting clerks, gas station attendants, or others to assist him in drawing or draw for him a line map with approximate distances and major landmarks. 2. By Dec. 15, Jim will score at least 70% on practice exams, administered under actual conditions.
Employment & Other Not needed at this time. Jim intends to enroll in auto mechanic training at LCC and is on track for a regular diploma. He is now taking auto shop and is doing well.		

The Secretary of Education has acknowledged that some IEP components, especially goals and objectives, may not be appropriate for all transition services (FR 44847, discussion of 34 CFR 300.346 (1997)). No IEP team should use time or energy trying to fit transition needs and services into a format including annual goals and objectives unless it truly makes sense to do so. Focus on the student's needs and how the school can address them.

Developing a Behavioral Intervention Plan (BIP) Component of the IEP

The IDEA now requires that the IEP include a behavioral intervention plan (BIP) for every disabled student whose behavior impedes his or her learning or that of others. Of course, this includes all students who are removed from their current placement to an alternative setting or excluded from school for more than ten days. The 1997 Amendments can be read to require a BIP for any suspension, however brief it may be. The U.S. Office of Education has taken the position that a BIP is required only for exclusions longer than ten days. This difference requires close watching, and we recommend erring on the side of providing a BIP rather than failing to provide it.

The BIP component of the IEP must be based upon a functional assessment of behavior. A functional analysis of behavior requires collecting data across settings on the events that precede (i.e., antecedents) and those that follow (i.e., consequences) the behavior of concern, so interventions can be developed to change the form or rate of the behavior or to teach alternative behaviors. The BIP must include positive behavioral interventions, strategies, and supports to address behaviors that interfere with learning. As appropriate, regular education teachers must assist in determining these positive interventions and strategies. The first step, of course, is to determine the problem behavior(s) and their frequency. The next step is to examine the antecedents and consequences in order to plan prevention and interventions.

The Texas law firm of Walsh, Anderson, Brown, Schulze, and Aldridge, P.C. (1997) has developed a behavioral intervention plan format that facilitates tracking such frequently occurring antecedent events as requests or directives from the teacher, provocation by peers, academic activity, and an unstructured setting or activity. Their list of likely past consequences that have followed problem behaviors includes positive social reinforcement from others, detention, removal from the classroom, suspension, or being sent to the principal's office.

The key portions of the BIP are: (1) the specification of targeted behaviors to be increased (e.g., time on task) or decreased (e.g., talking out without permission); and (2) the intervention strategies (including positive strategies) to be used, based upon the analysis of what elicits and/or maintains the problem behavior(s).

Figure 27 presents the Walsh et al. (1997) list of positive strategies (both antecedent and consequent) and consequences not always viewed as positive. Many teacher preparation programs have, in the past, failed to teach the use of positive behavioral interventions. The IDEA's new focus on these interventions in BIPs may be instrumental in remedying this serious deficiency.

Figure 27
Positive Behavioral Strategies and Consequences

Positive Behavioral Strategies for Increasing Prosocial Behaviors	Consequences Reasonably Calculated to Improve Behavior and Enable a Student to Receive Instruction
A. Remove distractors B. Provide a structured environment C. Set well-defined limits, rules, and task expectations D. Establish consistent routine E. Simplify activities F. Allow enough time to process information G. Use visual cues and supports H. Offer choices I. Set easily attainable daily goals J. Premack principle (if you do your <u>work task</u>, you may have <u>a reward</u>) K. Earn activities/privileges L. Planned ignoring of minor inappropriate behavior M. Provide frequent feedback concerning appropriateness of behavior N. Verbal reminders O Stand near the student P. Provide nonverbal signal for appropriate behavior Q. Positive reinforcers (List: _____) R. Point system S. Home-school reward system T. Behavior graphs U. Coach in problem-solving situations V. Role play consequences of behavior W. Teach alternative behaviors X. Contract for appropriate behavior Y. Teach social skills—direct instruction in prosocial behaviors Z. Set up and reinforce social interactions AA. Praise behaviorally appropriate students BB. Work completion contracts CC. Use timer for self-monitoring of on-task behavior DD. Direct overactivity into productive tasks within or outside the classroom (errands, performance tasks) EE. Frequent verbal reinforcement for appropriate behavior FF. Help student to use language (communication system) to label and communicate feelings GG. Permit student to remain in a quiet, nonthreatening, nonstimulating place in order to regain control when upset (a safe area) HH. Permit student to engage in physical activities II. Other:_____ JJ. Other:_____	*Consequences should be determined based upon the functioning level of the student and the severity of the behavior(s) exhibited.* 1. Review consequences before behavior escalates 2. Signal nonverbal disapproval 3. Ask student to practice appropriate response 4. Allow for peer pressure 5. Withhold earned activities/privileges 6. Response cost contracting 7. Offer student choice of changing behavior or going to "cooling off" area 8. Teacher-initiated "cooling off" period 9. Physical escort 10. Principal-student conference 11. Administrative behavioral contract 12. Use conflict management and mediation steps 13. Referral to counselor for anger control/replacement training 14. After-school detention 15. Lunch detention 16. In-school suspension for _____ period 17. In-school suspension for _____ days 18. In-school suspension up to ten school days w/o IEP meeting 19. Suspension for up to three consecutive days w/o IEP meeting 20. Other:_____ 21. Other:_____ 22. Other:_____

The Three-Step IEP Process Illustrated

Mike's case illustrates the three step IEP process. Mike is a seven-year old who has average intelligence and is legally blind. First, his unique characteristics/needs were described as follows:

1. Makes inappropriate gestures (e.g., hands clasped in air over head, shaking arms) dozens of times per hour.

2. Calls children names, speaks very negatively to others (e.g., "You're dumb," "You stink") and uses inappropriate vulgar and sexual vocabulary many times daily.

3. Is noncompliant with reasonable requests and suggestions from peers and adults several times daily.

4. Has a progressive visual condition which currently requires the use of Braille and ongoing mobility training.

The IEP team quickly agreed they could cluster characteristics #1-3 together and that the appropriate district service was a behavioral change plan using some combination of reinforcement of incompatible behaviors and perhaps response cost. The team agreed the behavior expert who serves Mike's building would develop such a plan within one week, and it would be put into his IEP. The goal for the behavioral plan was to bring all three kinds of behavior to an acceptable level by mid-year. The group agreed that within two weeks Mike would be participating in a fully implemented plan and that within one month all undesirable behaviors would be decreased by more than half. And so on.

The team agreed that Mike needed Braille instruction, and the IEP also provided for a volunteer back-up person to Braille his materials and for an itinerant specialist who would make daily visits to Mike's class. The goal was for Mike to continue to perform in all academic content areas at an average level. Objectives for that goal specified a timeline for increasing the speed and accuracy of Mike's Braille reading and writing.

Daily mobility training was agreed to with a goal of independent travel within the school. The first objective was for Mike to learn the layout of his new school building in one month. Sub-objectives (not required by law, but sometimes useful) were to learn, within two weeks, the routes from the school bus stop to the office, to his classroom, to the restroom, and back to the classroom.

In the best of worlds, all IEP teams would see as clearly and agree as professionally as Mike's did.

Examples of Educationally Useful IEPs

Several examples of partial IEPs or excerpts from IEPs follow. Each is based upon a real student whose parents had either requested a hearing or had actually been to hearing. These are pre-1998 IEPs so they do not reflect the new requirement of showing location of services. Nor are they intended to show anything but the true heart of the IEP—the needs, services, and goals.

Joe

Joe (see Figures 28a and b) earned no credits in ninth grade except in weightlifting. Even though he has above average intelligence, he has severe problems related to ADD (attention deficit disorder) and/or learning disabilities. The school told him to leave since he never handed in work and had failed all his classes. After staying away for three years, he is now returning to school. His rural high school has only seven teachers, very limited access to specialists, and fewer than 40 students. Joe's (partial) IEP reflects his real school world.

Figure 28a
Joe

Unique Educational Needs and Characteristics	Special Education, Related Services, Supplemental Aids & Services, Assistive Technology, Program Modifications, Support for Personnel	Present Levels Of Performance (PLOPs), Measurable Annual Goals, & Short-Term Objectives or Benchmarks • To enable student to participate in the general curriculum • To meet other needs resulting from the disability
(including how the disability affects the student's ability to progress in the general curriculum)	*(including frequency, duration, & location)*	*(including how progress toward goals will be measured)*
1. Joe needs more time to complete written assignments.	1. Adjust amount of work required (e.g., selected questions, page limits) and/or extend time for completion (e.g., for essays and content area assignments). Services begin immediately and continue throughout the year.	PLOP: Joe has been out of school for three years. Completed virtually no assignments during 9th grade.
2. Because of his attention deficits and difficulties, Joe needs frequent access to a low-distraction environment.	2.1 Provide in-classroom seating away from high distractions. 2.2 Provide an alternative workplace for independent work (e.g., study hall, library, resource room). Services begin immediately and continue throughout the year. 2.3 Provide inservice to all teachers on attention deficit disorder (by Oct. 3).	Objectives: 1. Within one month, Joe will complete 50% of his assignments with grade of "C" or better. 2. Within three months, Joe will complete 80% or more of his assignments with a "C" or better. 3. For the remainder of the year, Joe will maintain at least a "C" or better in all classes.
3. Joe needs assistance with oral and written directions.	3.1 Provide Joe with tape, tape recorder, and headphones, and instruct him in using this equipment unobtrusively in any classroom setting (by Oct. 3). 3.2 Classroom teachers will condense lengthy directions into steps and will write directions and assignments on chalkboard, wall chart, overhead transparency, handout, etc. Services begin immediately and continue throughout the year.	Goal: Joe will complete classroom assignments satisfactorily.

Figure 28b

Unique Educational Needs and Characteristics (including how the disability affects the student's ability to progress in the general curriculum)	Special Education, Related Services, Supplemental Aids & Services, Assistive Technology, Program Modifications, Support for Personnel (including frequency, duration, & location)	Present Levels of Performance (PLOPs), Measurable Annual Goals, & Short-Term Objectives or Benchmarks • To enable student to participate in the general curriculum • To meet other needs resulting from the disability (including how progress toward goals will be measured)
4. Joe doesn't know how to approach teachers to seek assistance.	4. Provide direct instruction in teacher approach behaviors. Services begin Sept. 5 and continue through Nov. 15.	PLOP: Joe never approaches teachers. Objectives: 1. Within one month, Joe and two of his teachers will agree he is interacting more, and more appropriately, with teachers. 2. Within three months, Joe and four of his teachers will agree he is "appropriate" in his interactions with teachers. Goal: Joe will seek assistance appropriately.
5. Joe is very disorganized, does not keep track of due dates, assignments, etc.	5. Provide appropriate materials and specific instruction in establishment and maintenance of an organizational system that includes a notebook and a calendar/checklist system. Services 10 minutes/day, Sept. 5-10.	PLOP: See characteristic. Objectives: 1. Within one week, Joe will physically organize a notebook with dividers for each class and use a calendar to track assignments, due dates, etc. Joe will check these daily with staff person. 2. By six months, Joe will independently use organized notebook and calendar list. Goal: Joe will successfully use organizing aids such as a notebook and calendar.
6. Joe needs to learn to deal with peers who tease him.	6. Provide instruction using appropriate assertive behaviors when teased. Services one hour weekly, Sept. 5-Nov. 15.	PLOP: Once or twice daily, Joe reacts inappropriately to peer teasing. Objectives: 1. Within two weeks, in role playing situations, Joe will respond appropriately to staged teasing. 2. Within six weeks, Joe will respond successfully in confrontations with peers 50% of the time (self-monitoring). 3. Within six months, Joe will respond successfully in confrontations with peers 100% of the time (self-monitoring), and the confrontations will be much less frequent. Goal: Joe will react appropriately to peers.

Curt

Curt (see Figures 29a, b, and c) is a ninth grade low achiever who was considered by the district to be a poorly motivated, disciplinary problem student with a "bad attitude." His parents recognized him as a very discouraged, frustrated student who had learning disabilities, especially in language arts.

Figure 29a
Curt

Unique Educational Needs, Characteristics, and Present Levels of Performance (PLOPs)	Special Education, Related Services, Supplemental Aids & Services, Assistive Technology, Program Modifications, Support for Personnel	Measurable Annual Goals & Short-Term Objectives or Benchmarks • To enable student to participate in the general curriculum • To meet other needs resulting from the disability
(including how the disability affects the student's ability to progress in the general curriculum)	*(including frequency, duration, & location)*	*(including how progress toward goals will be measured)*
Present Level of Social Skills: Curt lashes out violently when not able to complete work, uses profanity, and refuses to follow further directions from adults.

Social Needs:
• To learn anger management skills, especially regarding swearing
• To learn to comply with requests | 1. Teacher and/or counselor consult with behavior specialist regarding techniques and programs for teaching skills, especially anger management.

2. Provide anger management instruction to Curt. Services 3 times/week, 30 minutes.

3. Establish a peer group which involves role playing, etc., so Curt can see positive role models and practice newly learned anger management skills. Services 2 times/week, 30 minutes.

4. Develop a behavioral plan for Curt which gives him responsibility for charting his own behavior.

5. Provide a teacher or some other adult mentor to spend time with Curt (talking, game playing, physical activity, etc.). Services 2 times/week, 30 minutes.

6. Provide training for the mentor regarding Curt's needs/goals. | <u>Goal:</u> During the last quarter of the academic year, Curt will have 2 or fewer detentions for any reason.
Obj. 1: At the end of the 1st quarter, Curt will have had 10 or fewer detentions.
Obj. 2: At the end of the 2nd quarter, Curt will have had 7 or fewer detentions.
Obj. 3: At the end of the 3rd quarter, Curt will have had 4 or fewer detentions.

<u>Goal:</u> Curt will manage his behavior and language in a reasonably acceptable manner as reported by faculty and peers.
Obj. 1: At 2 weeks, asked at the end of class if Curt's behavior and language were acceptable or unacceptable, 3 out of 6 teachers will say "acceptable."
Obj. 2: At 6 weeks, asked the same question, 4 out of 6 teachers will say "acceptable."
Obj. 3: At 12 weeks, asked the same question, 6 out of 6 teachers will say "acceptable." |

Figure 29b

Unique Educational Needs, Characteristics, and Present Levels of Performance (PLOPs)	Special Education, Related Services, Supplemental Aids & Services, Assistive Technology, Program Modifications, Support for Personnel	Measurable Annual Goals & Short-Term Objectives or Benchmarks To enable student to participate in the general curriculum To meet other needs resulting from the disability
(including how the disability affects the student's ability to progress in the general curriculum)	*(including frequency, duration, & location)*	*(including how progress toward goals will be measured)*
Study Skills/Organizational Needs: How to read text Note taking How to study notes Memory work Be prepared for class, with materials Lengthen and improve attention span and on-task behavior Present Level: Curt currently lacks skill in all these areas.	1. Speech/lang. therapist, resource room teacher, and content area teachers will provide Curt with direct and specific teaching of study skills, i.e. Note taking from lectures Note taking while reading text How to study notes for a test Memorization hints Strategies for reading text to retain information 2. Assign a "study buddy" for Curt in each content area class. 3. Prepare a motivation system for Curt to be prepared for class with all necessary materials. 4. Develop a motivational plan to encourage Curt to lengthen his attention span and time on task. 5. Provide aide to monitor on-task behaviors in first month or so of plan and teach Curt self-monitoring techniques. 6. Provide motivational system and self-recording form for completion of academic tasks in each class.	**Goal:** At the end of academic year, Curt will have better grades and, by his own report, will have learned new study skills. **Obj. 1:** Given a 20-30 min. lecture/oral lesson, Curt will take appropriate notes as judged by that teacher. **Obj. 2:** Given 10-15 pgs. of text to read, Curt will employ an appropriate strategy for retaining info.—i.e., mapping, webbing, outlining, notes, etc.—as judged by the teacher. **Obj. 3:** Given notes to study for a test, Curt will do so successfully as evidenced by his test score. **Goal:** Curt will improve his on-task behavior from 37% to 80% as measured by a qualified observer at year's end. **Obj. 1:** By 1 month, Curt's on-task behavior will increase to 45%. **Obj. 2:** By 3 months, Curt's on-task behavior will increase to 60%. **Obj. 3:** By 6 months, Curt's on-task behavior will increase to 80% and maintain or improve until end of the year.

Figure 29c

Unique Educational Needs, Characteristics, and Present Levels of Performance (PLOPs) *(including how the disability affects the student's ability to progress in the general curriculum)*	Special Education, Related Services, Supplemental Aids & Services, Assistive Technology, Program Modifications, Support for Personnel *(including frequency, duration, & location)*	Measurable Annual Goals & Short-Term Objectives or Benchmarks • To enable student to participate in the general curriculum • To meet other needs resulting from the disability *(including how progress toward goals will be measured)*
Academic Needs/Written Language: Curt needs strong remedial help in spelling, punctuation, capitalization, and usage. Present Level: Curt is approximately 2 grade levels behind his peers in these skills.	1. Provide direct instruction in written language skills (punctuation, capitalization, usage, spelling) by using a highly structured, well-sequenced program. Services provided in small group of no more than four students in the resource room, 50 minutes/day. 2. Build in continuous and cumulative review to help with short-term rote memory difficulty. 3. Develop a list of commonly used words in student writing (or use one of many published lists) for Curt's spelling program.	*Goal:* Within one academic year, Curt will improve his written language skills by 1.5 or 2 full grade levels. Obj. 1: Given 10 sentences of dictation at his current level of instruction, Curt will punctuate and capitalize with 90% accuracy (checked at the end of each unit taught). Obj. 2: Given 30 sentences with choices of usage, at his current instructional level, Curt will perform with 90% accuracy. Obj. 3: Given a list of 150 commonly used words in writing, Curt will spell with 90% accuracy.

Adaptations to Regular Program:
• In all classes, Curt should sit near the front of the class.
• Curt should be called on often to keep him involved and on task.
• All teachers should help Curt with study skills as trained by spelling/language specialist and resource room teacher.
• Teachers should monitor Curt's work closely in the beginning weeks/months of his program.

Aaron

Aaron (see Figure 30) is a third grader with some troubling behavior, poor reading comprehension, and very poor handwriting.

Figure 30
Aaron

Unique Educational Needs and Characteristics	Special Education, Related Services, Supplemental Aids & Services, Assistive Technology, Program Modifications, Support for Personnel	Present Levels of Performance (PLOPs), Measurable Annual Goals, & Short-Term Objectives or Benchmarks • To enable student to participate in the general curriculum • To meet other needs resulting from the disability
(including how the disability affects the student's ability to progress in the general curriculum)	*(including frequency, duration, & location)*	*(including how progress toward goals will be measured)*
1. Aaron talks and draws inappropriately about monsters, torture, blood, etc.	1. Behavioral intervention, including: a. Behavior contract — To be implemented immediately b. Social skills program — One hour weekly for three months, beginning 9/20/97 c. In-room display of appropriate work	PLOP: 10-20 times daily Obj. 1: No more than twice daily by 10/1/97 Obj. 2: No more than once weekly by 10/15/97 Goal: Appropriate talking and drawing
2. Aaron makes many errors in reading and doesn't seem to recognize that the errors interfere with proper comprehension.	2. Remedial reading with emphasis on accuracy of decoding and monitoring comprehension — 30 minutes daily, beginning 9/15/97	PLOP: Reads 3rd grade material at 80-100 WPM with 5-12 errors and 30% accuracy on factual questions. Obj. 1: Reduce errors to 0-2 at 50-80 WPM by 11/1/97 Obj. 2: Read 3rd, grade material at 80-100 WPM with 0-2 errors by 12/15/97 with 70% accuracy on factual questions Goal: Grade level decoding and comprehension
3. Aaron has great difficulty in attempting cursive writing.	3. Timed manuscript probes (only legible letters to be counted) self-selected contingencies — Minimum two 1-minute probes daily Implemented immediately and continuing throughout the school year	PLOP: 8-10 legible manuscript letters per minute Obj. 1: 15-20 per minute by 11/15/97 Obj. 2: 20-25 per minute by 3/15/98 Goal: 35 per minute by 6/1/98

Megan

Megan (see Figure 31) is a ten-year old child who functions cognitively at about a four-year old level. She has Down Syndrome and is being educated in a regular class at her parents' insistence. The few components shown are but a small fraction of those in her complete IEP.

Figure 31
Megan

Unique Educational Needs, Characteristics, and Present Levels of Performance (PLOPs) *(including how the disability affects the student's ability to progress in the general curriculum)*	Special Education, Related Services, Supplemental Aids & Services, Assistive Technology, Program Modifications, Support for Personnel *(including frequency, duration, & location)*	Measurable Annual Goals & Short-Term Objectives or Benchmarks • To enable student to participate in the general curriculum • To meet other needs resulting from the disability *(including how progress toward goals will be measured)*
Megan has difficulty remembering daily routines: 1. Lunch (remembering hot or cold), taking medication, notes from home	Design a daily routine pocket board: • Lunch pocket—blue for cold, red for hot. • Note pocket for notes from home. • Medication pocket to put card into when she has taken medication. • Reward pocket for notes from teacher and reward tickets to be traded for prize from menu.	**Goal:** Independently use the daily routine board within one month. **Obj. 1:** Each day for one week, Megan will use the board with teacher's assistance. **Obj. 2:** Each day for the second week, Megan will use the routine board with only one reminder.
2. Has difficulty finding her books and locating the correct page.	Color code Megan's books so she can easily identify them. Put a marker in Megan's book before class so she can find her place.	**Goal:** Megan will locate her own books and find her place without any assistance in one week.
3. Gets lost in the building.	Make a game of finding her way from one location to another—teacher visual clues. Have Megan star or mark on a map all the paths she has mastered.	**Goal:** Megan will find her way to any point in the building within six months. **Obj.:** Megan will learn to find her way from one given point to another each week. Examples: Classroom to restroom, playground to classroom, lunchroom to classroom, etc.
Present level: Needs constant attention and reminders to complete any of the tasks listed above.		

These IEPs aren't perfect. But they are better, and that's what we want—**better IEPs**.

More Needs (PLOPs), Services, and Goals ala 1998

Academic (see Figures 32a and b) and nonacademic (see Figures 33a and b) components from several fictional students' IEPs show a range of characteristics, services, and goals, and different ways of presenting them. The students' profiles are all based on well-known lawsuits and depict the students' needs as described in the courts' decisions. For each, the rest of the IEP component indicates either what the court actually required, or what we believe it should have, or a combination.

Figure 32a
Partial IEP Academic Examples

Unique Educational Needs, Characteristics, and Present Levels of Performance (PLOPs) *(including how the disability affects the student's ability to progress in the general curriculum)*	Special Education, Related Services, Supplemental Aids & Services, Assistive Technology, Program Modifications, Support for Personnel *(including frequency, duration, & location)*	Measurable Annual Goals & Short-Term Objectives or Benchmarks • To enable student to participate in the general curriculum • To meet other needs resulting from the disability *(including how progress toward goals will be measured)*
JAMES		
James is a very bright 16-year old who is functionally illiterate, i.e., cannot distinguish "ladies" from "gentlemen" on doors. By shrewd guessing and a few sight words he can score from 1st to high 2nd grade on comprehension tests. His word attack skills are few, random, and ineffective.	Intensive, systematic, synthetic phonics reading instruction, 1:1 or small group (no more than 4) with a teacher or aide trained in the methodology used. Minimum one hour daily, plus same methodology to be used in all language arts areas consistently. Resource room and classroom.	End 1st 9 weeks: James will be able to decode all regular CVC words at 50 WPM/0 errors End 2nd 9 weeks: James will write and read the Dolch 220 End 3rd 9 weeks: James will read from 3rd grade material at 60 WPM/ 0-2 errors End 4th 9 weeks: James will score above 3.5 grade equivalent on 2 standardized reading tests.
RAFAEL		
Rafael is a 9-year old who has Down Syndrome. He lacks understanding of the alphabetic principle and is unable to associate any letters, other than t and m, with their sounds. He is easily distracted from any task by sound or movement.	1:1 Tutoring in a multisensory sound-symbol association method 15 minutes twice daily before noon in a small, quiet, distraction-free room.	Goal: Given flash cards with the letters, R. will be able to produce the main, regular sound for all short vowels, consonants, & digraphs with 100% accuracy, and when given each sound by the teacher, R. will be able to print the corresponding letter(s) legibly Obj. 1: By Nov. 1 R. will demonstrate s-s, as above, for f, m, s, r, t, a, i, l Obj. 2: By Jan 15 R. will (ditto) b, c, p, h, k, n, and o. wh, ch Obj. 3: By Mar. 15 R. will (ditto) remainder, including e and u
JEREMY		
Jeremy lacks understanding of the processes of multiplication and division and does not know the multiplication facts beyond x2. PLOP: Jeremy scored 10 correct problems out of 100 on the district comprehensive test of multiplication and division.	1. 20 minutes per school day, small group (< 5) instruction with remedial math specialist in the resource room. 2. Computerized drill and practice in multiplication and division for 15 minutes each school day.	GOAL: By the end of the school year, Jeremy will be able to complete 85% of multiplication and division problems correctly on the district math test. OBJ. #1: By Nov. 15 Jeremy will be able to complete a test of two-digit multiplication with at least 22 out of 25 score. OBJ. #2: By Feb. 15 Jeremy will be able to complete a test of simple division with at least a 22 out of 25 score.

Figure 32b

Unique Educational Needs, Characteristics, and Present Levels of Performance (PLOPs) *(including how the disability affects the student's ability to progress in the general curriculum)*	Special Education, Related Services, Supplemental Aids & Services, Assistive Technology, Program Modifications, Support for Personnel *(including frequency, duration, & location)*	Measurable Annual Goals & Short-Term Objectives or Benchmarks • To enable student to participate in the general curriculum • To meet other needs resulting from the disability *(including how progress toward goals will be measured)*
TARAH		
Tarah's expressive language skills are underdeveloped although she scores in the average range on nonlanguage measures of intelligence. She doesn't initiate conversation and answers questions with 1- or 2-word sentences. She has a spoken vocabulary of approximately 50-100 words. Her articulation is only slightly delayed (r, l not yet perfected) at the age of 7.	One-to-one direct instruction in vocabulary provided by a speech and language pathologist (SLP) three times per week/20 min. a session. Small group. SLP-led discussions with same-age peers twice per week/20 min. a session.	**Goal:** Tarah will initiate conversation with peers at least twice per day. 1. By November, Tarah will initiate a conversation with peers or with an adult on at least one occasion per week as monitored by teacher, instructional assistants, parent volunteers, recess teachers, special ed. teacher, or speech and language pathologist. 2. By March, Tarah will initiate conversation with same-age peers during speech class, or during work or play activities at least once per day.
R.S.		
R.S. needs a quiet, structured learning environment with minimal distractions. He currently can spell an average of 3 words from a 3rd grade list of 50 selected words.	Provide a quiet, structured learning environment with minimal distractions. Provide 1:1 direct instruction in spelling 5 days per week for 15 minutes each day.	R.S. will spell 45 of 50 selected 3rd grade words by the end of the year. Short-term: • By the end of the first quarter, R.S. will correctly spell 15 of 50 words. • By the end of the second quarter, R.S. will correctly spell 30 of 50 words.
TODD		
Todd's reading level is between the 4th and 5th grade level. His oral reading fluency rate is 70 words per minute with 5-6 errors, in 4th grade material.	Small group instruction from a reading specialist 30 minutes per day in a resource room beginning November 24, 1997 until November 23, 1998.	**STO 1:** In 3 one-minute timed passages, Todd will increase his oral reading fluency to 90 words/minute with 2-3 errors by 4/24/98. **STO 2:** In 3 one-minute timed passages, Todd will increase his oral reading fluency to 110 words/minute with 1-2 errors by 9/24/98. **Goal:** In 3 one-minute timed passages, Todd will increase his oral reading fluency to 150 words/minute with 0-1 errors by 11/23/98.
DANIEL		
Daniel recognizes one color by name (red). Daniel recognizes one shape by name (circle). Daniel recognizes the words for two spatial concepts (on, under).	One-to-one direct instruction in color, shape, & spatial concepts by the classroom aide for 10 minutes per day in the classroom, beginning September 1, 1997.	**Goal:** Daniel will follow directions, answer questions, or identify objects to demonstrate understanding of 21 new concepts without error. **STO 1:** Daniel will point on request to brown, white, orange, purple, yellow, blue, green, black by 4/24/98 with no errors. **STO 2:** Daniel will point on request to diamond, oval, square, star, heart by 6/3/98. **STO 3:** Daniel will demonstrate an understanding of near, far, above, next to, in front of, behind, beside by 11/23/98 without error.

Figure 33a
Partial IEP Nonacademic Examples

Unique Educational Needs, Characteristics, and Present Levels of Performance (PLOPs) *(including how the disability affects the student's ability to progress in the general curriculum)*	Special Education, Related Services, Supplemental Aids & Services, Assistive Technology, Program Modifications, Support for Personnel *(including frequency, duration, & location)*	Measurable Annual Goals & Short-Term Objectives or Benchmarks • To enable student to participate in the general curriculum • To meet other needs resulting from the disability *(including how progress toward goals will be measured)*
JEFF		
10-15 violent or near violent outbursts for 10-15 min. weekly	Response cost contract in all classes	G: Zero inappropriate outbursts by end of year O1: By Dec., <3 for 5 minutes weekly O2: By Mar., <1 monthly
JED		
Jed talks to and interrupts other students during study time an average of 10 times per half hour.	Allow peer pressure to operate. Lunch detention after 5 interruptions.	Goal: By the end of the school year, Jed will not talk to other students during quiet work times. Obj. #1: By Jan. 15, Jed will interrupt others no more than 5 times per half hour. Obj. #2: By March 15, Jed will interrupt other students no more than 2 times per half hour.
RAFAEL		
Has outbursts in the classroom. These outbursts consist of yelling, biting, and kicking. Outbursts occur at least twice per day for a duration of approximately 20 min. PLOP: When Rafael is asked to follow teacher directions that he perceives as difficult, the tantrum behavior is observed. Rafael follows teacher directions, without tantrum, within 5 seconds no more than 35% of the time.	Physical escort to cooling off area.	Rafael will follow teacher directions within 5 seconds without verbal and physical tantrums. Objective 1: Rafael will follow teacher directions without tantrums in 70% of the opportunities for 3 consecutive days by 11/14. Objective 2: Rafael will follow teacher directions without tantrums in 90% of the opportunities for 5 consecutive days by 1/15.

Figure 33b

Unique Educational Needs, Characteristics, and Present Levels of Performance (PLOPs) *(including how the disability affects the student's ability to progress in the general curriculum)*	Special Education, Related Services, Supplemental Aids & Services, Assistive Technology, Program Modifications, Support for Personnel *(including frequency, duration, & location)*	Measurable Annual Goals & Short-Term Objectives or Benchmarks • To enable student to participate in the general curriculum • To meet other needs resulting from the disability *(including how progress toward goals will be measured)*
DANIEL		
Doesn't know how to play with others. He grabs toys away from other children, has difficulty sharing. PLOP: During parallel play with a small group of peers Daniel grabs toys away from a classmate at least 6 times daily (twice in each of 3 ten-minute periods).	A behavioral plan (attached) that addresses cooperation and sharing. Teach alternative behaviors. Frequent verbal reinforcement for appropriate behavior.	When playing in a small group of peers, Daniel will verbally ask his peers if he can borrow their toys and will not grab. Obj 1: When playing in a small group of peers, and verbally cued during play time, Daniel will ask his peers if he can borrow their toys half of the time by 1/15. Obj 2: When playing in a small group of peers, and hearing a verbal announcement about toy sharing before the play session begins, Daniel will ask his peers if he can borrow their toys 3/4 of the time for 5 consecutive days by 5/15.
R.G.		
R.G. worries excessively about his schoolwork. PLOP: R.G. asks to go to the school nurse at least once per day because of stress-related stomach pains or headaches.	In-school "stress-proof" group counseling once per week for 1/2 hour with school psychologist. Behavioral contract with self-selected reinforcements.	Goal: By the end of the school year, R.G. will not miss any school time because of stress. Obj #1: By 12/15, R.G. will not ask to go to the nurse more than 3x/week. Obj #2: By 2/28, R.G. will not ask to go to the nurse more than once/week.
TODD		
Todd is a social isolate at recess and lunch, seldom if ever seen interacting with other students.	(a) A volunteer "special buddy" will be assigned to draw Todd into socialization with others. (b) Playground & cafeteria monitors will comment favorably to Todd about his interactions after such are observed, at least once daily.	Goal: Todd will interact easily with peers at a rate not noticeably different from that of his peers. Obj. By Dec. 15 he will participate in at least 2 observed appropriate interactions during each recess and lunch. Obj. By Mar. 15 he will (ditto) at least 4 interactions
W.G.		
W.G. has trouble staying in his seat during class. He gets up and wanders during both instruction and independent work time. Currently he leaves his seat an average of 10-15 times per hour.	Place W.G.'s desk where the teacher can monitor him. Give W.G. 3 cards per day that allow him to get out of his seat during independent work time only. A token economy will be used to increase uninterrupted seat time.	W.G. will get out of his seat <3 times (during independent work) per day. (1) By the end of the first quarter, W.G. will decrease getting out of his seat by half. (2) By the end of the second quarter, W.G. will get out of his seat <4 times per day.

IEPs for §504 Students?

Section 504 of the Rehabilitation Act of 1973 prohibits discrimination against persons on the basis of disability. Confusion abounds about what kind of IEP or IEP-like document, if any, students are entitled to when they are eligible for §504 but not for the IDEA. Many schools treat some students who have been diagnosed as having ADD (attention deficit disorder) or ADHD (ADD with hyperactivity) as though they were eligible only under §504. Other §504 eligible, but not IDEA eligible students could include the temporarily disabled and students who have diabetes, epilepsy, asthma, etc. and do not need special education. Please note that if a student has a disability which necessitates special education, the chances are very high that he or she is eligible under **both** the IDEA and §504.

The basic educational entitlement under §504 is to:

> … regular or special education and related aids and services that: (i) are designed to meet the individual educational needs of handicapped persons as adequately as the needs of nonhandicapped persons are met, and (ii) are based upon adherence to procedures … (34 CFR 104.33 (b)(l)).

An IDEA IEP is one legally recognized way to meet this §504 requirement. A school might choose this option just because it is familiar. That is a perfectly okay way to proceed.

A widespread and deeply held misconception is that §504 eligible students are entitled **only** to "reasonable accommodations." How and why this misconception arose is outside the scope of this discussion—suffice it to say it was and is an erroneous reading of §504. In fact, the §504 entitlement is exactly as quoted above, i.e., to education and services that meet the needs of the disabled student as well as the needs of nondisabled students are met. That is what §504 is about—nondiscrimination on the basis of disability.

§504 does not describe the process or document to be used in specifying the services required for nondiscrimination. Parents and school personnel should focus on the result of meeting needs and should use the simplest possible written document. Sometimes providing only "reasonable accommodations" would be sufficient to meet the "as adequately as nondisabled" standard. Oftentimes it would not.

One fascinating §504 case involves a student whose disability was a blood condition that could cause fatal bleeding from a minor injury. The student accidentally cut herself in art class and, in a fearful outburst, she uttered expletives. The school expelled her for misconduct. The student successfully sought an injunction to prevent the expulsion. The court found that the student's behavior was caused by her disability and concluded that, under these circumstances, §504 required leniency in applying the student conduct code. The court cautioned that "... blind adherence to policies and standards resulting in a failure to accommodate a person with a disability is precisely what the Americans with Disabilities Act of 1990 and the Rehabilitation Act of 1973 are intended to prevent" (*Thomas v. Davidson Academy*, 846 F. Supp. 611 (M.D. Tenn., 1994)).

In other words, §504 requires public and private schools that receive or benefit from Federal monies to provide such services—including making accommodation, changes, or allowances—as to result in the student not being disadvantaged or discriminated against solely because of a disability.

As illustrated in this chapter, many details must be attended to in preparing a good IEP. However, it is vital to keep in mind, as the courts do, that the main point of having an IEP at all is to spell out in a clear, measurable way how a child's program is to be individualized to meet his or her unique needs. Figure 34 presents the bare bones essentials of a good IEP. Any IEP that embodies these five virtues will be educationally useful.

Figure 34

IEP VIRTUES

I. FULL AND EQUAL PARENTAL PARTICIPATION

II. TRULY INDIVIDUALIZED TO FIT THE STUDENT

III. PRESENT LEVELS OF PERFORMANCE (PLOPS) AND NEEDS/CHARACTERISTICS CAREFULLY SPECIFIED

IV. ALL SERVICES, MODIFICATIONS, AND SUPPORTS TO MEET THE STUDENT'S NEEDS FULLY DETAILED

V. GOALS AND OBJECTIVES MEASURABLE, REAL, AND TAKEN SERIOUSLY

IEP Myths, Battles, and Truths

Teachers, administrators, academics, parents, and other interested persons engage in lively debate about special education policy and practice. This healthy discourse encourages research on effective practices and inspires people to examine important social and political issues relating to the education of children with disabilities. Unfortunately, it also sometimes obscures the line that separates wishes, opinions, and beliefs from the requirements of the law, and it often leads to disputes between parents and schools. In this chapter, we will examine several contentious areas of the IDEA and identify what that law actually says.

Free Appropriate Public Education

Nothing is more fundamental to the IDEA than the principle that every child with a qualifying disability is entitled to a free appropriate public education (FAPE). The meanings of free and public are reasonably clear, but the meaning of appropriateness frequently causes confusion. How does one know what is appropriate?

Appropriate does not necessarily mean ideal. Though schools might wish to afford every child an opportunity to maximize his or her potential, the IDEA does not require this. The U. S. Supreme Court has held:

> … Insofar as a State is required to provide a handicapped child with a "free appropriate public education," we hold that it satisfies this requirement by providing personalized instruction with sufficient support services to permit the child to benefit educationally from that instruction. Such instruction and services must be pro-

vided at public expense, must meet the State's educational standards, must approximate the grade levels used in the State's regular education, and must comport with the child's IEP. In addition, the IEP, and therefore the personalized instruction, should be formulated in accordance with the requirements of the Act and, if the child is being educated in the regular classrooms of the public education system, should be reasonably calculated to enable the child to achieve passing marks and advance from grade to grade (*Board of Education v. Rowley*, 458 U.S. 176 (1982)).

Benefit

Questions about what constitutes educational benefit lie at the center of countless cases. How should one measure benefit, from what perspective does one measure, and is a little benefit enough? Educational benefit must be judged on an individual basis. A Federal district court in Texas has explained that:

> A child, an individual with unique problems, cannot be held up and compared to nondisabled children. This is simply not a reasonable standard. The question is, does [the child] receive any meaningful benefit from his individual education plan? … [W]hether this benefit would be meaningful for his age peers is irrelevant (*El Paso Indep. Sch. Dist. v. Robert W. by Judy W.*, 898 F.Supp. 442 (W.D. Tex., 1995)).

Some courts have held that the phrase "reasonably calculated" is the key to the benefit inquiry. In *Fuhrmann v. East Hanover Bd. of Educ.*, the 3rd Circuit stated, "Our understanding of *Rowley* [is] that the measure and adequacy of an IEP can only be determined as of the time it is offered to the student, and not at some later date" (993 F.2d 1031 (3rd Cir., 1993)). In a similar vein, the 1st Circuit has taken the position that " … the issue is not whether the IEP was prescient enough to achieve perfect academic results" but whether it was "objectively reasonable" when it was developed. The court said evidence of "actual educational results" was relevant but not conclusive (*Roland M. v. Concord School Committee*, 910 F.2d 983, 992 (1st Cir., 1990)).

The 9th Circuit recently held that "… the correct standard for measuring educational benefit under the IDEA is not merely whether the placement is 'reasonably calculated to provide the child with educational benefits,' but rather, whether the child makes progress toward the goals set forth in her IEP" (*County of San Diego v. California Special Educ. Hearing Office*, 93 F.3d 1458 (9th Cir., 1996)). Regardless of whether they purport to look forward or backward, it appears that courts look to results when determining whether a child is receiving educational benefit.

Amount of Progress

This leads to the question of how much progress is sufficient to indicate that a child is receiving educational benefit. Some courts caution that *Rowley* requires only limited benefit, but even those cases do not stand for the proposition that merely placing a disabled student in a classroom and providing some kind of instruction satisfies the IDEA requirements. The 11th Circuit Court of Appeals said that the IDEA " … would be worthless if handicapped children received no benefit from the 'free appropriate public education' … " (*J.S.K. v. Hendry County Sch. Bd.*, 941 F.2d 1563 (11th Cir., 1991)).

Neither social promotion nor slight achievement indicate sufficient progress. In a case involving a dyslexic student whose school failed for years to identify his disability and provide an appropriate program despite his chronic academic failure, the 4th Circuit asserted that "Congress did not intend that a school system could discharge its duty … by providing a program that produces some minimal academic advancement, no matter how trivial" *(Hall v. Vance County Bd. of Educ.*, 774 F.2d 629 (4th Cir., 1985)). The 3rd Circuit shares this view, holding that the IDEA " … calls for more than a trivial educational benefit" *(Polk ex rel. Polk v. Central Susquehanna Intermediate Unit No. 16*, 853 F.2d 171 (3rd Cir., 1988)).

The IDEA sets a Chevrolet standard, not a Cadillac. Be careful, though, not to mistake this for a Yugo standard. An IEP need not provide a superior education, but it must offer real educational benefit.

Although the IDEA establishes a minimum standard, state laws may offer greater educational benefits to students with disabilities. Several states have laws that require schools to maximize students' capabilities, ensure opportunities for students to reach their full potential, or otherwise suggest a higher standard than that set by Federal law. A full survey of state law is beyond the scope of this book, but districts and parents should be aware of their state requirements that may exceed those of the IDEA.

IEP Contents

Erroneous understandings about what goes into an IEP are widespread, and many IEPs lack important pieces of information or misconceive the proper relationships among the components. This leads to unnecessary work and, often, to discord between parents and schools. The U.S. Supreme Court has stated that an IEP is " ... a comprehensive statement of the educational needs of a handicapped child and the specially designed instruction and related services to be employed to meet those needs" (*Burlington Sch. Comm. v. Massachusetts Dept. of Educ.*, 471 U.S. 359 (1985)). Too often, when educators think about IEPs, they focus on what the student will do—the lists of annual goals and objectives—and they pay scant attention to what the school will do to help the student achieve those goals. This is a mistake! This notion not only pointlessly increases the paperwork burden for teachers, who laboriously reshape curriculum outlines into objectives, but also diverts attention from the indispensable machinery of the IEP—the special education, related services, and supplementary aids and services through which the school will address the needs of the student.

Special education is " ... specially designed instruction, at no cost to parents, to meet the unique needs of a child with a disability" (20 USC §1401(25)). Related services include " ... transportation, and such developmental, corrective, and other supportive services ... as may be required to assist a child with a disability to benefit from special education" (20 USC §1401(22)). Supplementary aids and services are " ... aids, services, and other supports that are provided in regular education classes or other education-related settings to enable children with disabilities to be educated with nondisabled children to the maximum extent appropriate" (20 USC §(29)). The specifics of what special education, related services, and supplementary aids and services are included in an IEP must be determined individually, depending upon that child's unique needs.

Addressing Students' Unique Educational Needs

The IDEA mandates careful assessment of the unique educational needs of students with disabilities and provision of services to meet those needs. The detailed procedures governing evaluation (20 USC §1414(a), (b), & (c)) and IEP content (20 USC §1414(d)(1)(A) & (3)(A) &(B)) show Congress intended a comprehensive needs analysis and a coordinating complement of services. Vague, general, or categorical statements of needs and boilerplate statements of service provision will not suffice.

Balancing the need to identify and meet all of a student's unique needs with the minimal requirement that an IEP be reasonably calculated to confer benefit can be difficult. Nevertheless, IEP teams should not ignore any of a disabled student's identified needs on the dubious premise that they must assure only that the student receive some benefit. In the event of a legal challenge, an IEP team must be able to explain its delineation of the student's needs and how they were met. Perhaps the key is how critical the need is to a student's ability to benefit from educational services. We recommend that every IEP meeting begin with the team listing the student's unique needs, as this helps the team to focus on the task at hand. It clarifies what else the IEP must include and saves the time that might otherwise be wasted on listing services and goals that are unrelated to any of the student's needs.

Methodology

Whether methodology should appear in IEPs was debated for years, but the question now has an answer. In the House Committee Report on the IDEA Amendments of 1997, Congress expressly stated that " ... while teaching and related service methodologies or approaches are an appropriate topic for discussion and consideration by the IEP team during IEP development or annual review, they are not expected to be written into the IEP" (H. Rep. No. 105-95 (1997, pp. 100 -101)). This does not mean that methodology has become a nonissue. It is closely entwined with appropriateness, and it will continue to be an issue with children who don't progress satisfactorily with methods their schools have selected.

Issues of methodology seem to have a uniquely polarizing effect, and many disputes between schools and parents about methodology have ended up in the courtroom. Litigation is a poor way of resolving these disputes, as courts are very reluctant to deal with this issue. In *Rowley*, the U.S. Supreme Court explained this reticence: "Courts must be careful to avoid imposing their view of preferable educational methods upon the States. The primary responsibility ... for choosing the educational method ... was left to state and local educational agencies in cooperation with the parents ... " (458 U.S. at 207). In the following sentence, the court noted that the IDEA expressly requires states to disseminate and adopt promising educational practices. Clearly, the Court assumed that schools know about and employ effective, research-based methodologies. In fact, it added that

" ... in the face of such a **clear statutory directive** [authors' emphasis], it seems unlikely Congress intended courts to overturn a State's choice of appropriate educational theories ... " (458 U.S. at 208)

It would appear, in light of *Rowley*, that when it can be shown that a school has violated that clear statutory directive by choosing methodologies unrelated to current knowledge of effective research-based practice, the school's choice should not be granted preference. However, no court has yet linked the school's right to select methodology to its responsibility to employ data-based, effective methodology.

The typical judicial analysis of methodology is limited, as described by one Federal court:

> The court agrees with Plaintiff that questions of methodology cannot be analyzed as separate and distinct from the question of whether an IEP provides an appropriate education for an individual handicapped child. However, integrating questions of methodology into the analysis of the appropriateness of a proposed IEP does not change the standard regarding the appropriateness of the overall educational plan (*Brougham v. Yarmouth*, 823 F.Supp. 9 (1993)).

Another Federal court decision, involving a preschool child with autism, had no trouble seeing an inextricable connection between methodology and appropriateness:

> ... The evaluations make clear that E, an autistic child with his own individual problems, needs to continue in an intensive ABA [Lovaas method] program to encourage and develop his ability to relate with others and to derive an "educational benefit" from group socialization like the music, gym, and cooking classes and group interactions provided by AMAC. From the record, it is clear that the IEP did not provide E with the specialized educational and related services that would meet his unique needs as an autistic child, particularly, in light of the fact that at the time AMAC was recommended as the appropriate placement for E, it had neither a one-to-one aide for him nor an appropriate ABA program in place to meet his needs (*Mr. X. v. New York State Educ. Dept.*, 975 F.Supp. 546 (1997)).

Sometimes a critical mass of expert testimony will persuade a court that a student needs a particular instructional method. One Federal court recently found a district's proposed IEP inappropriate because it did not provide the " ... intensive program of individualized, integrated, multisensory, sequential [phonics] training" that several dyslexia specialists testified was essential to the student's ability to benefit from an educational program (*Evans v. Board of Educ. of Rhinebeck Cent. Sch. Dist.*, 930 F.Supp 83 (1996)).

A student's disability category may be a significant determinant of whether a court will closely examine a district's choice of methodology. Parents of students with autism have been more successful than most in methodology-based challenges, perhaps because autistic children often make no measurable progress at all when the school chooses unsystematic or loosely structured methods. At the other end of the spectrum are students with learning disabilities, many of whom can get by regardless of what methods their teachers use. If a district can show that a student appears to receive **some** benefit, as indicated by passing (often just barely) grades, a court will often look no further.

A particularly interesting realm of methodology-related disputes involves students with hearing impairments. In these cases, choice of methodology implicates politics as well as program efficacy. One faction of the deaf community rejects the "medical model" of deafness and its associated stigma. Instead, they identify themselves as a distinct cultural group with its own language, American Sign Language (ASL). Another faction, which seeks integration with the nondeaf population, prefers lip-reading and spoken language. In most disputes thus far, parents have preferred oral communication rather than sign language or "Total Communication," which uses both sign and spoken languages. Hearings officers and courts, using the *Rowley* benefit analysis, have deferred to school districts' choices (see, e.g., *Logue by Logue v. Shawnee Mission Pub. Sch. Unified Sch. Dist. No. 512*, 25 IDELR 587 (D.Kan., 1997)). It seems possible that "deaf culture" proponents could construct a persuasive argument that hearing impaired children constitute a linguistic minority and need instruction in their own language, but this has not yet happened.

Special Education and Related Services

An IEP must include statements of what the district will do to meet each of the child's needs. Among the items to be included are special education, related services, supplementary aids and services, program modifications, and personnel support the child will need to "advance appropriately" toward annual goals, to "be involved and progress in" the general curriculum, and to participate with other disabled and nondisabled children (20 USC §1414(d)(1)(A)(iii)).

The increased emphasis in the IDEA on the general curriculum points out the need for districts to provide adequate training and support for regular classroom teachers. As important as the need for these teachers to acquire new skills is the need for them to understand their legal obligations to students with disabilities. Some teachers may prefer not to modify their curriculum, instruction, or assessment, but they cannot with impunity refuse to implement the terms of a student's IEP. One teacher learned this lesson the hard way. A high school history teacher in West Virginia (*Doe v. Withers*, 20 IDELR 422 (West Va. Cir. Ct., 1993)) refused to honor a student's IEP provision that tests were to be administered orally. The parents sued, and the teacher lost. The jury awarded damages of $15,000, including $10,000 in punitive damages.

The modifications that can and should appear on IEPs and be properly implemented are well-illustrated by the case of a 15-year old diagnosed as a high functioning autistic student (TX SEA, *Richardson Indep. Sch. Dist.*, 21 IDELR 333 (1994)). His IEP contained a list of classroom modifications that included:

> … highlighting important information, utilizing shortened directions and assignments, provision of summaries or reviews, changing the format of written materials, preferential seating, flexible time allowances, small group instruction, modification of mastery levels on essential elements, and use of multiple choice or word banks instead of fill-in-the-blank questions.

The IEP also provided for activities to help the student improve his social skills. Additionally, the student's regular and special education teachers were required to communicate with one another about his assignments and any problems he might be having.

An IEP must list all modifications and accommodations necessary to meet the student's educational needs and must specify details about how these services are to be implemented. In a recent case involving a student with a visual impairment, cerebral palsy, anxiety, and several other health problems, the district's IEP was found inappropriate because it failed to address many of the student's physical, psychological, social, mobility, and organizational needs. An appeals panel sharply criticized the district's inadequate description of accommodations:

> The section on specially designed instruction is pathetic in its paucity. The District offers a microcassette recorder ostensibly to facilitate note taking in class. However, the District offers Christopher neither training in strategies to takes notes nor strategies to use the recorder ….
>
> … Noticeably absent … are other areas of need. Because of both visual and motor problems, Christopher writes slowly and has limited endurance. Yet, we find no accommodations offered for limited ability to produce written responses: There are

no shortened assignments, no oral tests or reports suggested; there are no opportunities to move around the room or vary activities to reduce fatigue .... [H]is IEP notes that he "needs to strengthen organizational skills." However, there is no specially designed instruction (or annual goals or short-term objectives) targeting organizational skills. Christopher has difficulty in social situations. There is no specific instruction targeting this need ....

Too often, IEP goals and objectives are thought of as an evaluation of the student because they are formulated in terms of student behavior. A ruling from a Maine hearing is most instructive and helpful in understanding the correct focus of an IEP (ME SEA, *Sch. Admin. Dist. #25*, 20 IDELR) 1316 (1994)) where an IEP was found deficient in that it lacked several features essential for providing a FAPE to a high school student with brittle diabetes. First, the behavioral plan on the IEP was not individualized. Further,

> ... that plan does not reflect his current level of performance; it contains no goals and objectives to move him from where he is now to where he needs to be. **Nor does it state how the school will get him there** [authors' emphasis] .... [It] fails to state how P's attendance, leaving class, not being in class or in study hall, completion of assigned work, and make-up work will be addressed.

This ruling makes a vital point that is seldom well-understood. After finding that the teachers have selected appropriate adaptive strategies and modifications, the hearing officer points out that those **strategies and modifications should be the focus of the goals and objectives**. This is exactly correct and illustrates precisely the IEP process urged in this volume. Goals and objectives are formulated to evaluate the effectiveness of the district services. A Federal district court has also explained the proper relationship between behavioral objectives and educational interventions:

> ... [T]he absence of specific behavioral objectives in Cory's ... IEPs makes it virtually impossible ... to evaluate whether particular educational strategies are actually having an impact (*Chris D. and Cory M. v. Montgomery Co. Bd. of Ed.*, 753 F.Supp. 922 (M.D. Ala., 1990)).

Behavioral management plans, if needed, should be included in IEPs, and they aren't just for children with emotional disturbance, a point on which there has been some confusion in the past. Several years ago, an Alabama hearing officer concluded that a student diagnosed with ADHD, serious emotional disturbance, and other health impairments was not entitled to a behavioral plan. The district had argued that no plan was needed even though the 11-year old student had a history of disruptive behavior, noncompliance, temper outbursts, fighting, kicking, and throwing objects, plus a suicide threat. The student had passed most of his classes, so the hearing officer reasoned that the IEP provided the student with more than de minimus benefits and was, therefore, appropriate. One can only wonder what advantage the district saw in refusing to provide a behavioral plan, regardless of whether it was legally required.

The IDEA Amendments of 1997 have eliminated any ambiguity on this point. If a child's behavior impedes "... his or her learning or that of others," the IEP team must "... consider, when appropriate, strategies, including positive behavioral interventions ... and supports to address that behavior" (20 USC §1414(d)(3) (B)(i)).

An Office for Civil Rights (OCR) ruling highlights a different (and appalling) behavior management issue. In this case, a school bus driver punished a student in violation of the terms of his IEP. The IEP provided that problem conduct in several settings, including the school bus, would result in the loss of certain privileges. The bus driver, who did not know about the IEP, "disciplined" the student by choking, slapping, and suspending him from the bus. Needless to say, the OCR found the district had violated the law (*West Las Vegas (NM) Sch. Dist.*, 20 IDELR 1358 (OCR, 1993)).

IEPs also should provide for any assistive technology devices and services the child needs (20 USC §1414(d)(3)(B)(v)). The IEP team decides whether a child needs assistive technology and in what settings the child should use such devices and services (57 Fed. Reg. 44794, 44845 (Sept. 29, 1992)). An assistive technology device is "... any item, piece of equipment, or product system ... that is used to increase, maintain, or improve functional capabilities of a child with a disability" (20 USC §1401(1)). An assistive technology service is "... any service that directly assists a child with a disability in the selection, acquisition, or use of an assistive technology device" (20 USC §1401(2)).

If a child's IEP includes assistive technology devices or services, the district must provide them at no cost to the parents (22 IDELR 373 (OSEP, 1994)). Eyeglasses are considered assistive technology devices, and they too must be provided at no cost if the child needs them in order to receive FAPE (*Bachus*, 22 IDELR 629 (OSEP)). If, through negligence or abuse, a child loses or damages a publicly owned assistive technology device, state law may require reimbursement from the parents, but parents are not responsible for damage due to normal wear and tear (25 IDELR 1212 (OSEP, 1997)).

Another thorny IEP issue is extended school year (ESY), which provides supplementary schooling outside of the normal school day, week, or year for students who need it. ESY should be included in an IEP along with other special education and related services, if appropriate.

In *Reusch v. Fountain*, 21 IDELR 1107 (D.MD., 1994), the Federal district court examined the ESY services of a Maryland school district and found significant substantive and procedural abuses. These errors are common in many school districts. A major problem centered around failure to inform parents about their child's possible entitlement to ESY services and failure to enable the parents to obtain these services. The district didn't notify the parents of a denial of summer school services until late in the school year, thus precluding the parents from obtaining a due process hearing before the summer program ended. Another error was the district's reliance on a regression/recoupment formula for determining eligibility. The formula requires quantification of how much the student will regress without ESY and/or how long would it take that student to make up lost ground. The court ordered the district to consider additional factors in determining ESY eligibility. Finally, the ESY program was a standardized, fixed length, with no provision for fitting duration to students' individual needs.

The bottom line is that a child with a disability is entitled to any and all services necessary to allow him or her to benefit from education, and all needed services must be included in the IEP.

IEP Development Procedures

The U.S. Supreme Court held that one of the definitional elements of "appropriate" in FAPE is that the school must follow the IDEA procedural requirements (*Rowley*). Does or should this mean that any procedural deficiency in IEP development can be the basis for declaring a program inappropriate? School administrators reasonably fear the affirmative answer that would leave districts vulnerable to endless litigation and expense. Fortunately for school districts, the trend in administrative and judicial decisions is to distinguish harmless errors from those procedural flaws that truly prejudice parents' and children's rights. A typical view is that of the Federal district court in *Myles S. v. Montgomery Co. Bd. of Ed.*, 824 F.Supp. 1549 (M.D. Ala., 1993), which concluded:

> ... [T]he court appreciates the concern expressed by Myles' parents but also finds that the school system has substantially complied with the provisions of the IDEA. The court notes that Myles' parents were correct in asserting that the school system did not technically comply with a number of IDEA provisions. As these failures to comply were not done in bad faith, still allowed Myles to benefit educationally, and still allowed Myles' parents to participate fully and effectively in Myles' education, no relief is warranted for these past violations. However, prospective relief is warranted in part.

Of course, school districts are not off the hook for gross violations of the IDEA procedural violations. The 9th Circuit provided a thorough, if lengthy, review of this issue in *W.G. v. Target Range Sch. Dist. #23*, 960 F.2d 2479 (9th Cir., 1992), where it held that procedural errors invalidated the IEP and entitled the parents to reimbursement for the private schooling they had obtained. The court itemized the district's procedural errors: (1) they developed the IEP without participation of the parents, the regular classroom teacher, or a representative of the private school the student attended; (2) they proposed a method to which the parents objected and refused to consider any alternatives; and (3) they ignored the recommendations of persons knowledgeable about the student in proposing a placement. The court discussed other grounds on which a court could find an IEP fatally flawed:

> When a district fails to meet the procedural requirements of the Act by failing to develop an IEP in the manner specified, the purposes of the Act are not served, and the district may have failed to provide a FAPE. The significance of the procedures provided by the IDEA goes beyond any measure of a child's academic progress during the period at issue. As the Court in *Rowley* said, "Congress placed every bit as much emphasis upon compliance with procedures giving parents and guardians a large measure of participation" at every step "as it did upon the measurement of the resulting IEP" (*Rowley*, 458 U.S. at 205-06).
>
> Target Range's arguments that the parents are to blame because they left the IEP meeting, did not file a dissenting report, and led the district to believe that the principal problem was transportation, are without merit. The parents had no obligation to file a dissent. The school district was well aware of their concerns, which ranged from specific methodologies and student-teacher ratios to transportation and the location of special education services ....

Target Range contends that a … 4th Circuit case, *Denton*, 895 F.2d at 982, stands for the proposition that only those procedural faults that cause a student loss of benefits result in a denial of FAPE. We disagree ….

Because we hold that Target Range failed to develop the IEP according to the procedures required by the Act and by Montana law, we need not address the question of whether the proposed partial IEP was reasonably calculated to enable R.G. to receive education benefits (*W.G. v. Board of Trustees of Target Range Sch. Dist.*, 960 F.2d 1479 (9th Cir., 1992)).

The IEP and Special Education Placement

One of the most widely and seriously violated procedural requirements related to IEPs is that a placement decision must be based upon a completed IEP. The only exception to this rule is when the student is in an ongoing private placement. Since the IEP team for a child attending private school includes a representative of that school, the placement is a given going into the meeting.

The IDEA regulations simply and clearly state that the IEP must be "… in effect before special education and related services are provided to a child" (34 CFR §300.342(b)(1)). The courts understand that this is true "… even if that requires meeting with the parents during the summer" (*Myles S.*).

IEP Team

Contrary to practice in some schools, the IEP team is not merely a formality, convening briefly to sign an IEP created by a teacher in isolation. The IDEA is very specific about who must be on the team, and the members are supposed to work in concert to develop the IEP.

Parents head the list, and excluding them would be a fatal flaw. A common district failure, and a risky one, is not having a proper district representative at every IEP meeting. An equally serious, but rare, reason for invalidating an IEP is that a required teacher was not present. An Office of Special Education and Rehabilitative Services (OSERS) ruling advises that a district "… must ensure the attendance at all IEP meetings of both the child's teacher and a representative of the public agency, other than the child's teacher, who is qualified to provide, or to supervise the provision of, special education" 18 IDELR 1036 (OSERS, 1992). Under the new requirements of the 1997 Amendments, at least one regular education teacher and at least one special education teacher must be on the team. Given the increased emphasis on access to the general curriculum, and a likely increase in attention to supplementary aids and services to enable students to participate in mainstream classes, the regular teacher may play a prominent role on the team.

The IDEA grants sole authority to the IEP team for deciding what services a child will receive. The district representative on the team must have the authority to commit district resources without threat of veto from a higher ranking administrator. Nevertheless, administrators sometimes inappropriately intervene in the IEP process. One such situation led an Iowa school district to a richly deserved due process hearing:

> … [T]he process of IEP development is one of attempting to arrive at consensus about appropriate special education programs. In order to achieve that result, no one person on an IEP team can or should exercise greater power or voice in the decision making than anyone else on the team. (See 34 CFR Part 300, Appendix C, No. 26, p. 82 (1993)). Yet, that is not what happened here. District administrators, admittedly strangers to [ ]'s IEP process, arrived on the scene at a time when the rest of the team was in the process of formulating a significant change in the IEP. The other educators on the team, and [ ]'s parents, were headed toward a determination that [ ] should not be graduated and, instead, should be provided additional educational programming. That IEP team effort was effectively stopped when the administrators usurped the decision-making process. The two administrators stood firm, without educational justification, backed only by their interpretation of District policy, saying that it required that [ ] graduate and effectively end the District's responsibility for her education (IS SEA, *Mason City Comm. Sch. Dist.*, 21 IDELR 248 (1994)).

IEP Process

Who's in charge? The question naturally arises about what decision-making process an IEP team is supposed to use. Consensus is the ideal way for districts and parents to reach agreement on the provisions of the IEP, but sometimes that ideal is difficult to achieve. Parents are equal partners with school personnel on the team, and their information and concerns about their child are important considerations. Ultimately, however, the district is responsible for ensuring the child has an IEP that constitutes FAPE. If the team fails to reach consensus, the district must give parents prior written notice of its proposals and/or refusals regarding the child's program and placement. The parents may accept or reject the district offer, and if they disagree, they may seek resolution of the dispute through mediation or due process hearing (34 CFR Part 300, Appendix C, Question 9 (1998)). The earlier Appendix C advised that, in case of an impasse at the IEP meeting, the parents and district should agree to an interim measure or to having the child remain in the current placement until the disagreement is resolved (34 CFR Part 300, Appendix C, Question 35 (1981)).

In an intriguing ruling, OSEP declared that only the decisions the IEP team makes about legally required components of an IEP are binding. All other IEP team decisions or agreements may be overruled unilaterally by an agency administrator (*Hehir*, 20 IDELR 1222 (1993)). This poses no threat to IEP team decisions on special education, related services, or any of the other components that must be included in the IEPs. It does, however, suggest that IEP team members should be cautious in discussing and making decisions about issues peripheral to the IEP.

Consequences of Inappropriate IEPs

District personnel rightly fear a finding that a student's program is inappropriate. Such a finding can be very expensive if the child's parents have given up on the public school and unilaterally placed their child in a private school. The U.S. Supreme Court in *Florence Co. Sch. Dist. Four v. Carter* (510 U.S. 7 (1993)) has spoken loudly and clearly to those districts that fear the financial consequences of failing to make a free, appropriate program available to a student who has a disability:

> … [P]ublic education authorities who want to avoid reimbursing parents for the private education of a disabled child can do one of two things: give the child a free appropriate public education in a public setting, or place the child in an appropriate private setting of the State's choice. This is IDEA's mandate, and school officials who conform to it need not worry about reimbursement claims ….

> … [O]nce a court holds that the public placement violated IDEA, it is authorized to "grant such relief as the court determines is appropriate" (20 USC . §1415(e)(2)). Under this provision, "equitable considerations are relevant in fashioning relief," *Burlington*, 471 U.S. at 374, and the court enjoys "broad discretion in so doing," *id.*, at 369. Courts fashioning discretionary equitable relief under IDEA must consider all relevant factors ….

Reimbursement for Costs of Private School

Reimbursement for a unilateral placement in a private school is one of the most common equitable remedies available to parents when a district fails to make FAPE available to their child. In *Burlington Sch. Comm. v. Mass. Dept. of Ed.*, 471 U.S. 359 (1985), the U.S. Supreme Court established the rule that parents are entitled to reimbursement for private school placements when the district's offered program is not appropriate under *Rowley* and the private placement is appropriate. The Court added, in *Carter*, that private placement need not be state approved and suggested (but did not hold) that reimbursement may be limited to that which is reasonable.

The 9th Circuit dealt with this issue in *Capistrano Unified Sch. Dist. v. Wartenberg*, 59 F.3d 884, 891 (9th Cir., 1995). A 16-year old boy with learning disabilities, attention deficit disorder, and a conduct disorder had a long history of school failure and behavioral problems. After the district offered an IEP that seemed to provide even fewer services than the several previous unsuccessful IEPs, the parents enrolled their son in a private school and sought reimbursement from the district. The district alleged that their offered IEPs were appropriate and that the boy's continuing academic failures resulted from misbehavior rather than disability. After rejecting this theory, the court applied the *Burlington* test, and awarded full reimbursement of private school expenses to the parents. Particularly persuasive was the fact that, after years of dismal failure, the boy began making academic progress in the highly structured environment of the private school, which offered a high teacher-student ratio, teacher and classroom continuity throughout the day, and a comprehensive behavioral plan.

A Federal district court in Maryland awarded reimbursement to parents for tuition and tutoring at a private school when the public school's IEP was neither procedurally nor substantively correct. The school failed to develop an IEP until November 4 of the student's first grade year, even though the parents had requested an evaluation on May 17 and in early August the student had been diagnosed as dyslexic. The evidence also established that the IEP finally offered on November 4 was composed solely of pieces assembled from other IEPs, and the contents were not at all specific to the student (*Gerstmyer v. Howard Co. Pub. Sch.*, 20 IDELR 1327 (D.Md., 1994)).

Parents who unilaterally place their children in private schools do so at their own risk, as there is no guarantee of reimbursement. The 1997 Amendments provide that reimbursement may be reduced or denied:

(i) if—

(aa) At the most recent IEP meeting that the parents attended prior to removal of the child from the public school, the parents did not inform the IEP team that they were rejecting the placement proposed by the public agency to provide a free appropriate public education to their child, including stating their concerns and their intent to enroll their child in a private school at public expense; or

(bb) Ten business days (including any holidays that occur on a business day) prior to the removal of the child from the public school, the parents did not give written notice to the public agency of the information described in division (aa);

(ii) if, prior to the parents' removal of the child from the public school, the public agency informed the parents, through the notice requirements described in section 615(b)(7), of its intent to evaluate the child (including a statement of the purpose of the evaluation that was appropriate and reasonable), but the parents did not make the child available for such evaluation; or

(iii) upon a judicial finding of unreasonableness with respect to actions taken by the parents.

(iv) EXCEPTION- Notwithstanding the notice requirement in clause (iii)(I), the cost of reimbursement may not be reduced or denied for failure to provide such notice if—

(I) The parent is illiterate and cannot write in English;

(II) Compliance with clause (iii)(I) would likely result in physical or serious emotional harm to the child;

(III) The school prevented the parent from providing such notice; or

(IV) The parents had not received notice, pursuant to section 615, of the notice requirement in clause (iii)(I)(20 USC §1412(a)(10(C)(iii)&(iv)).

A recent 5th Circuit decision illustrates the risk parents incur when they seek reimbursement for unilateral placement in private school. In this case, the court applied a four-part test to the district's program, asking whether: (1) the program was individualized on the basis of the student's assessment and performance; (2) the program was administered in the least restrictive environment; (3) the services were provided in a coordinated and collaborative manner by the key "stakeholders"; and (4) whether positive academic and nonacademic benefits were demonstrated. The court quickly answered "yes" to the first three questions and then concluded that the answer to the fourth question was also "yes" because the child, who had attention deficit hyperactivity disorder (ADHD) and Tourette Syndrome, had earned passing grades and was able to engage in some routine tasks without supervision. The court not only denied reimbursement to the parents, but also ordered the parents to pay costs of litigation, a highly unusual result (*Cypress-Fairbanks Independent School District v. Michael F., 118 F.3d 245 (5th Cir., 1997)*).

Compensatory Education

If a student did not attend private school, tuition reimbursement is not an appropriate remedy for district failure to provide a FAPE. In several cases, the courts have held that compensatory education may be appropriate relief. In one such case, the district, in addition to other serious IDEA violations, had denied an aide to a student who could not attend school without one and thus deprived her of a FAPE for three years. When the student turned 22, the school claimed it had no further obligation to her. The court held that she was entitled to three years of compensatory education beyond her 22nd birthday and said the IEP team should determine the exact nature of those services (*Melvin v. Town of Bolton Sch. Dist.*, 20 IDELR 1189 (D.Vt., 1993)).

When a Pennsylvania district failed to provide the 108 individual, 30-minute speech and language therapy sessions that were on an IEP, the hearing appeals officer ordered that they be provided over the next four summers. If the student became eligible for extended school year (ESY) services in the future, those services would be in addition to the therapy sessions (PA SEA, *Philadelphia Sch. Dist.*, 21 IDELR 320 (1994)).

A Federal district court found that a Minnesota school district failed for two years to provide an appropriate program because the student's IEP did not include present levels of performance and did not address all of the student's individual needs. The court, however, refused to order reimbursement for the private school into which the parents had unilaterally placed their son because that school also failed to provide an appropriate program. Instead, the court awarded two years of compensatory education in the public school (*Brantley by Brantley v. Independent Sch. Dist. No. 625*, 26 IDELR 839 (D.Minn., 1997)).

Damages

Another possible consequence to districts for failure to provide FAPE is compensatory damages. Historically, courts have held that damages are not available under the IDEA because the statute does not expressly authorize the award of damages. Recently, in *Emma C. v. Eastin*, 26 IDELR 1140 (N.D. Cal., 1997), a Federal district court in California, holding that damages might be available, declined to dismiss a class action suit in which a group of children sought compensatory damages. The court looked at the IDEA section authorizing courts to "… grant such relief as the court determines is appropriate" (20 U.S.C. § 1415(e)(2)) and found no bar to damages. Furthermore, the court noted a U.S. Supreme Court decision holding that monetary damages were available under Title IX of the Education Amendments of 1972 (20 USC §§1681), a statute that also lacked specific authorization of damages. In that case, the Court said that "The general rule, therefore, is that absent clear direction to the contrary by Congress, the Federal courts have the power to award any appropriate relief in a cognizable cause of action brought pursuant to a Federal statute" (*Franklin v. Gwinnett County Pub. Sch.*, 503 U.S. 60 (1992)).

Conclusion

IEPs should be developed correctly both because of negative legal consequences when one doesn't and positive educational results when one does (see Figure 35). The successful IEP process begins with knowing the unique needs of the student, moves on to specifying the services that will be provided to address those needs, and concludes by writing goals and objectives that will be used to evaluate the services. It may not be as easy as 1-2-3, but it gets closer to that each time an IEP is prepared the right way, with the sole focus on successfully addressing the individual student's needs.

Figure 35

IEP
GOSPEL TRUTHS

A LEGALLY APPROPRIATE IEP IS
INDIVIDUALIZED AND REASONABLY
CALCULATED TO ALLOW THE STUDENT TO
RECEIVE EDUCATIONAL BENEFIT.

IEP DEVELOPMENT MUST PROCEED IN
ACCORDANCE BOTH WITH THE IDEA AND
WITH ITS REGULATIONS.

AN IEP THAT IS FLAWED IN SUBSTANCE OR
PROCEDURE EXPOSES A DISTRICT TO THE
RISKS OF LITIGATION AND SUCH EXPENSIVE
REMEDIES AS PRIVATE SCHOOL COSTS,
COMPENSATORY EDUCATION, OR EVEN
POSSIBLY DAMAGES.

IDEA Statute (1997)

20 USC §1414 Sec. 1414. Evaluations, Eligibility Determinations, Individualized Education Programs, and Educational Placements.

(a) Evaluations and Reevaluations.

(1) Initial Evaluations.

(A) In General. State educational agency, other State agency, or local educational agency shall conduct a full and individual initial evaluation, in accordance with this paragraph and subsection (b), before the initial provision of special education and related services to a child with a disability under this part.

(B) Procedures. Such initial evaluation shall consist of procedures—

(i)   To determine whether a child is a child with a disability (as defined in Section 1402(3)); and

(ii) To determine the educational needs of such child.

(C) Parental Consent.

(i)   In General. The agency proposing to conduct an initial evaluation to determine if the child qualifies as a child with a disability as defined in Section 1402(3)(A) or 602(3)(B) shall obtain an informed consent from the parent of such child before the evaluation is conducted. Parental consent for evaluation shall not be construed as consent for placement for receipt of special education and related services.

(ii) Refusal. If the parents of such child refuse consent for the evaluation, the agency may continue to pursue an evaluation by utilizing the mediation and due process procedures under Section 1415, except to the extent inconsistent with State law relating to parental consent.

(2) Reevaluations. A local educational agency shall ensure that a reevaluation of each child with a disability is conducted—

(A) If conditions warrant a reevaluation or if the child's parent or teacher requests a reevaluation, but at least once every three years; and

(B) In accordance with subsections (b) and (c).

(b) Evaluation Procedures.

(1) Notice. The local educational agency shall provide notice to the parents of a child with a disability, in accordance with subsections (b)(3), (b)(4), and (c) of Section 1415, that describes any evaluation procedures such agency proposes to conduct.

(2) Conduct of Evaluation. In conducting the evaluation, the local educational agency shall—

(A) Use a variety of assessment tools and strategies to gather relevant functional and developmental information, including information provided by the parent, that may assist in determining whether the child is a child with a disability and the content of the child's individualized education program, including information related to enabling the child to be involved in and progress in the general curriculum or, for preschool children, to participate in appropriate activities;

(B) Not use any single procedure as the sole criterion for determining whether a child is a child with a disability or determining an appropriate educational program for the child; and

(C) Use technically sound instruments that may assess the relative contribution of cognitive and behavioral factors, in addition to physical or developmental factors.

(3) Additional Requirements. Each local educational agency shall ensure that—

(A) Tests and other evaluation materials used to assess a child under this section—

(i)   Are selected and administered so as not to be discriminatory on a racial or cultural basis; and

(ii) Are provided and administered in the child's native language or other mode of communication, unless it is clearly not feasible to do so; and

(B) Any standardized tests that are given to the child—

(i)   Have been validated for the specific purpose for which they are used;

(ii) Are administered by trained and knowledgeable personnel; and

(iii) Are administered in accordance with any instructions provided by the producer of such tests;

(C) The child is assessed in all areas of suspected disability; and

(D) Assessment tools and strategies that provide relevant information that directly assists persons in determining the educational needs of the child are provided.

(4) Determination of Eligibility. Upon completion of administration of tests and other evaluation materials—

(A) The determination of whether the child is a child with a disability as defined in Section 1402(3) shall be made by a team of qualified professionals and the parent of the child in accordance with paragraph (5); and

(B) A copy of the evaluation report and the documentation of determination of eligibility will be given to the parent.

(5) Special Rule for Eligibility Determination. In making a determination of eligibility under paragraph (4)(A), a child shall not be determined to be a child with a disability if the determinant factor for such determination is lack of instruction in reading or math or limited English proficiency.

(c) Additional Requirements for Evaluation and Reevaluations.

(1) Review of Existing Evaluation Data. As part of an initial evaluation (if appropriate) and as part of any reevaluation under this section, the IEP team described in subsection (d)(1)(B) and other qualified professionals, as appropriate, shall—

(A) Review existing evaluation data on the child, including evaluations and information provided by the parents of the child, current classroom-based assessments and observations, and teacher and related services providers' observation; and

(B) On the basis of that review, and input from the child's parents, identify what additional data, if any, are needed to determine—

(i) Whether the child has a particular category of disability, as described in Section 1402(3), or, in case of a reevaluation of a child, whether the child continues to have such a disability;

(ii) The present levels of performance and educational needs of the child;

(iii) Whether the child needs special education and related services, or in the case of a reevaluation of a child, whether the child continues to need special education and related services; and

(iv) Whether any additions or modifications to the special education and related services are needed to enable the child to meet the measurable annual goals set out in the individualized education program of the child and to participate, as appropriate, in the general curriculum.

(2) Source of Data. The local educational agency shall administer such tests and other evaluation materials as may be needed to produce the data identified by the IEP team under paragraph (1)(B).

(3) Parental Consent. Each local educational agency shall obtain informed parental consent, in accordance with subsection (a)(1)(C), prior to conducting any reevaluation of a child with a disability, except that such informed parental consent need not be obtained if the local educational agency can demonstrate that it had taken reasonable measures to obtain such consent and the child's parent has failed to respond.

(4) Requirements if Additional Data Are Not Needed. If the IEP team and other qualified professionals, as appropriate, determine that no additional data are needed to determine whether the child continues to be a child with a disability, the local educational agency—

   (A) Shall notify the child's parents of—

      (i)   That determination and the reasons for it; and

      (ii) The right of such parents to request an assessment to determine whether the child continues to be a child with a disability; and

   (B) Shall not be required to conduct such an assessment unless requested by the child's parents.

(5) Evaluations Before Change in Eligibility. A local educational agency shall evaluate a child with a disability in accordance with this section before determining that the child is no longer a child with a disability.

Subsection (d) is not effective until July 1, 1998; however, (d)(6) was effective June 4, 1997.

(d) Individualized Education Programs.

(1) Definitions. As used in this title:

   (A) Individualized Education Program. The term "individualized education program" or "IEP" means a written statement for each child with a disability that is developed, reviewed, and revised in accordance with this section and that includes—

(i) A statement of the child's present levels of educational performance, including—

    (I) How the child's disability affects the child's involvement and progress in the general curriculum; or

    (II) For preschool children, as appropriate, how the disability affects the child's participation in appropriate activities;

(ii) A statement of measurable annual goals, including benchmarks or short-term objectives, related to—

    (I) Meeting the child's needs that result from the child's disability to enable the child to be involved in and progress in the general curriculum; and

    (II) Meeting each of the child's other educational needs that result from the child's disability;

(iii) A statement of the special education and related services and supplementary aids and services to be provided to the child, or on behalf of the child, and a statement of the program modifications or supports for school personnel that will be provided for the child—

    (I) To advance appropriately toward attaining the annual goals;

    (II) To be involved and progress in the general curriculum in accordance with clause (i) and to participate in extracurricular and other nonacademic activities; and

    (III) To be educated and participate with other children with disabilities and nondisabled children in the activities described in this paragraph;

(iv) An explanation of the extent, if any, to which the child will not participate with nondisabled children in the regular class and in the activities described in clause (iii);

(v)   (I) A statement of any individual modifications in the administration of State- or district-wide assessments of student achievement that are needed in order for the child to participate in such assessment; and

     (II) If the IEP team determines that the child will not participate in a particular State- or district-wide assessment of student achievement (or part of such an assessment), a statement of—

       (aa) Why that assessment is not appropriate for the child; and

       (bb) How the child will be assessed;

(vi) The projected date for the beginning of the services and modifications described in clause (iii), and the anticipated frequency, location, and duration of those services and modifications;

(vii) (I) Beginning at age 14, and updated annually, a statement of the transition service needs of the child under the applicable components of the child's IEP that focuses on the child's courses of study (such as participation in advanced placement courses or a vocational education program);

     (II) Beginning at age 16 (or younger, if determined appropriate by the IEP team), a statement of needed transition services for the child, including, when appropriate, a statement of the interagency responsibilities or any needed linkages; and

     (III) Beginning at least one year before the child reaches the age of majority under State law, a statement that the child has been informed of his or her rights under this title, if any, that will transfer to the child on reaching the age of majority under Section 1415(m); and

(viii) A statement of—

     (I) How the child's progress toward the annual goals described in clause (ii) will be measured; and

(II) How the child's parents will be regularly informed (by such means as periodic report cards), at least as often as parents are informed of their nondisabled children's progress, of—

(aa) Their child's progress toward the annual goals described in clause (ii); and

(bb) The extent to which that progress is sufficient to enable the child to achieve the goals by the end of the year.

(B) Individualized Education Program Team. The term "individualized education program team" or "IEP team" means a group of individuals composed of—

(i) The parents of a child with a disability;

(ii) At least one regular education teacher of such child (if the child is, or may be, participating in the regular education environment);

(iii) At least one special education teacher, or where appropriate, at least one special education provider of such child;

(iv) A representative of the local educational agency who—

(I) Is qualified to provide, or supervise the provision of, specially designed instruction to meet the unique needs of children with disabilities;

(II) Is knowledgeable about the general curriculum; and

(III) Is knowledgeable about the availability of resources of the local educational agency;

(v) An individual who can interpret the instructional implications of evaluation results, who may be a member of the team described in clauses (ii) through (vi);

(vi) At the discretion of the parent or the agency, other individuals who have knowledge or special expertise regarding the child, including related service personnel as appropriate; and

(vii) Whenever appropriate, the child with a disability.

(2) Requirement That Program Be in Effect.

(A) In General. At the beginning of each school year, each local educational agency, State educational agency, or other State agency, as the case may be, shall have in effect, for each child with a disability in its jurisdiction, an individualized education program, as defined in paragraph (1)(A).

(B) Program for Child Aged Three Through Five. In the case of a child with a disability aged three through five (or, at the discretion of the State educational agency, a two-year old child with a disability who will turn age three during the school year), an individualized family service plan that contains the material described in Section 1436, and that is developed in accordance with this section, may serve as the IEP of the child if using that plan as the IEP is—

(i) Consistent with State policy; and

(ii) Agreed to by the agency and the child's parents.

(3) Development of IEP.

(A) In General. In developing each child's IEP, the IEP team, subject to subparagraph (C), shall consider—

(i) The strengths of the child and the concerns of the parents for enhancing the education of their child; and

(ii) The results of the initial evaluation or most recent evaluation of the child.

(B) Consideration of Special Factors. The IEP team shall—

(i) In the case of a child whose behavior impedes his or her learning or that of others, consider, when appropriate, strategies, including positive behavioral interventions, strategies, and supports to address that behavior;

(ii) In the case of a child with limited English proficiency, consider the language needs of the child as such needs relate to the child's IEP;

(iii) In the case of a child who is blind or visually impaired, provide for instruction in Braille and the use of Braille unless the IEP team determines, after an evaluation of the child's reading and writing skills, needs, and appropriate reading and writing media (including an evaluation of the child's future needs for instruction in Braille or the use of Braille), that instruction in Braille or the use of Braille is not appropriate for the child;

(iv) Consider the communication needs of the child, and in the case of a child who is deaf or hard of hearing, consider the child's language and communication needs, opportunities for direct communications with peers and professional personnel in the child's language and communication mode, academic level, and full range of needs, including opportunities for direct instruction in the child's language and communication mode; and

(v) Consider whether the child requires assistive technology devices and services.

(C) Requirement With Respect to Regular Education Teacher. The regular education teacher of the child, as a member of the IEP team, shall, to the extent appropriate, participate in the development of the IEP of the child, including the determination of appropriate positive behavioral interventions and strategies and the determination of supplementary aids and services, program modifications, and support for school personnel consistent with paragraph (1)(A)(iii).

(4) Review and Revision of IEP.

(A) In General. The local educational agency shall ensure that, subject to subparagraph (B), the IEP team—

(i) Reviews the child's IEP periodically, but not less than annually to determine whether the annual goals for the child are being achieved; and

    (ii)   Revises the IEP as appropriate to address—

        (I)   Any lack of expected progress toward the annual goals and in the general curriculum, where appropriate;

        (II) The results of any reevaluation conducted under this section;

        (III) Information about the child provided to, or by, the parents, as described in subsection (c)(1)(B);

        (IV) The child's anticipated needs; or

        (V) Other matters.

  (B) Requirement With Respect to Regular Education Teacher. The regular education teacher of the child, as a member of the IEP team, shall, to the extent appropriate, participate in the review and revision of the IEP of the child.

(5) Failure to Meet Transition Objectives. If a participating agency, other than the local educational agency, fails to provide the transition services described in the IEP in accordance with paragraph (1)(A)(vii), the local educational agency shall reconvene the IEP team to identify alternative strategies to meet the transition objectives for the child set out in that program.

Subsection (d)(6) is effective June 4, 1997.

(6) Children With Disabilities in Adult Prisons.

  (A) In General. The following requirements do not apply to children with disabilities who are convicted as adults under State law and incarcerated in adult prisons:

    (i)   The requirements contained in Section 1412(a)(17) and paragraph (1)(A)(v) of this subsection (relating to participation of children with disabilities in general assessments).

    (ii) The requirements of subclauses (I) and (II) of paragraph (1)(A)(vii) of this subsection (relating to transition planning and transition services), do not apply with respect to such children whose eligibility under this part will end, because of their age, before they will be released from prison.

(B) Additional Requirement. If a child with a disability is convicted as an adult under State law and incarcerated in an adult prison, the child's IEP team may modify the child's IEP or placement notwithstanding the requirements of sections 1412(a)(5)(A) and 1414(d)(1)(A) if the State has demonstrated a bona fide security or compelling penological interest that cannot otherwise be accommodated.

(e) Construction.

Nothing in this section shall be construed to require the IEP team to include information under one component of a child's IEP that is already contained under another component of such IEP.

(f) Educational Placements.

Each local educational agency or State educational agency shall ensure that the parents of each child with a disability are members of any group that makes decisions on the educational placement of their child.

As last amended by Pub.L. 105-17 (June 4, 1997).

IDEA Regulations (Proposed)

34 CFR 300.340-300.351

Sec. 300.340 Definitions.

(a) As used in this part, the term individualized education program means a written statement for a child with a disability that is developed, reviewed, and revised in accordance with Secs. 300.341-300.351.

(b) As used in Secs. 300.347 and 300.348, participating agency means a State or local agency, other than the public agency responsible for a student's education, that is financially and legally responsible for providing transition services to the student.

(Authority: 20 U.S.C. 1401(11))

Sec. 300.341 State educational agency responsibility.

(a) Public agencies. The SEA shall ensure that each public agency develops and implements an IEP for each child with a disability served by that agency.

(b) Private schools and facilities. The SEA shall ensure that an IEP is developed and implemented for each child with a disability who—

(1) Is placed in or referred to a private school or facility by a public agency; or

(2) Is enrolled in a religiously-affiliated school or other private school and receives special education or related services from a public agency.

(Authority: 20 U.S.C. 1412(a)(4), (a)(10)(A) and (B))

Note: This section applies to all public agencies, including other State agencies (e.g., departments of mental health and welfare) that provide special education to a child with a disability either directly, by contract, or through other arrangements. Thus, if a State welfare agency contracts with a private school or facility to provide special education to a child with a disability, that agency would be responsible for ensuring that an IEP is developed for the child.

Sec. 300.342 When IEPs must be in effect.

(a) At the beginning of each school year, each LEA, SEA, or other State agency, shall have in effect, for each child with a disability within its jurisdiction, an individualized education program, as defined in Sec. 300.340.

(b) An IEP must—

    (1) Be in effect before special education and related services are provided to a child; and

    (2) Be implemented as soon as possible following the meetings described under Sec. 300.343.

(c) (1) In the case of a child with a disability aged three through five (or, at the discretion of the SEA a two-year old child with a disability who will turn age three during the school year), an IFSP that contains the material described in section 636 of the Act, and that is developed in accordance with Secs. 300.340-300.346 and 300.349-300.351, may serve as the IEP of the child if using that plan as the IEP is—

    (i) Consistent with State policy; and

    (ii) Agreed to by the agency and the child's parents.

    (2) In implementing the requirements of paragraph (c)(1) of this section, the public agency shall—

        (i) Provide to the child's parents a detailed explanation of the differences between an IFSP and an IEP; and

        (ii) If the parents choose an IFSP, obtain written informed consent from the parents.

(d) (1) All IEPs in effect on July 1, 1998 must meet the requirements of Secs. 300.340-300.351.

(2) The provisions of Secs. 300.340-300.350 that were in effect on June 3, 1997 remain in effect until July 1, 1998.

(Authority: 20 U.S.C. 1414(d)(2)(A) and (B), Pub. L. 105-17, sec. 201(a)(1)(C))

Note 1: It is expected that the IEP of a child with a disability will be implemented immediately following the meetings under Sec. 300.343. Exceptions to this would be if: (1) the meetings occur during the summer or a vacation period, unless the child requires services during that period, or (2) there are circumstances that require a short delay (e.g., working out transportation arrangements). However, there can be no undue delay in providing special education and related services to the child.

Note 2: Certain requirements regarding IEPs for students who are incarcerated in adult prisons apply as of June 4, 1997.

Note 3: At the time that a child with a disability moves from an early intervention program under Part C of the Act to a preschool program under this part, the parent, if the agency agrees, has the option, under paragraph (c) of this section, to allow the child to continue receiving early intervention services under an IFSP, or to begin receiving special education and related services in accordance with an IEP. Because of the importance of the IEP as the statutory vehicle for ensuring FAPE to a child with a disability, paragraph (c)(2) of this section provides that the parents' agreement to use an IFSP for the child instead of an IEP requires written informed consent by the parents that is based on an explanation of the differences between an IFSP and an IEP.

Sec. 300.343 IEP meetings.

(a) General. Each public agency is responsible for initiating and conducting meetings for the purpose of developing, reviewing, and revising the IEP of a child with a disability (or, if consistent with State policy and at the discretion of the LEA, and with the concurrence of the parents, an IFSP described in section 636 of the Act for each child with a disability, aged three through five).

(b) Timelines.

(1) Each public agency shall ensure that an offer of services in accordance with an IEP is made to parents within a reasonable period of time from the agency's receipt of parental consent to an initial evaluation.

(2) In meeting the timeline in paragraph (b)(1) of this section, a meeting to develop an IEP for the child must be conducted within 30 days of a determination that the child needs special education and related services.

(c) Review and revision of IEP. Each public agency shall ensure that the IEP team—

(1) Reviews the child's IEP periodically, but not less than annually, to determine whether the annual goals for the child are being achieved; and

(2) Revises the IEP as appropriate to address—

(i) Any lack of expected progress toward the annual goals described in Sec. 300.347(a), and in the general curriculum, if appropriate;

(ii) The results of any reevaluation conducted under this section;

(iii) Information about the child provided to, or by, the parents, as described in Sec. 300.533(a)(1);

(iv) The child's anticipated needs; or

(v) Other matters.

(Authority: 20 U.S.C. 1414(d)(3))

Note: For most children, it would be reasonable to expect that a public agency offer services in accordance with an IEP within 60 days of receipt of parental consent to initial evaluation.

Sec. 300.344 IEP team.

(a) General. The public agency shall ensure that the IEP team for each child with a disability includes—

(1) The parents of the child;

(2) At least one regular education teacher of the child (if the child is, or may be, participating in the regular education environment);

(3) At least one special education teacher, or if appropriate, at least one special education provider of the child;

(4) A representative of the LEA who—

    (i) Is qualified to provide, or supervise the provision of, specially designed instruction to meet the unique needs of children with disabilities;

    (ii) Is knowledgeable about the general curriculum; and

    (iii) Is knowledgeable about the availability of resources of the LEA;

(5) An individual who can interpret the instructional implications of evaluation results, who may be a member of the team described in paragraphs (a)(2) through (6) of this section;

(6) At the discretion of the parent or the agency, other individuals who have knowledge or special expertise regarding the child, including related service personnel as appropriate; and

(7) If appropriate, the child.

(b) Transition services participants.

(1) Under paragraph (a)(7) of this section, the public agency shall invite a student with a disability of any age if a purpose of the meeting will be the consideration of the statement of transition service needs or statement of needed transition services for the student under Sec. 300.347(b)(1).

(2) If the student does not attend the IEP meeting, the public agency shall take other steps to ensure that the student's preferences and interests are considered.

(3) (i) In implementing the requirements of paragraph (b)(1) of this section, the public agency also shall invite a representative of any other agency that is likely to be responsible for providing or paying for transition services.

    (ii) If an agency invited to send a representative to a meeting does not do so, the public agency shall take other steps to obtain participation of the other agency in the planning of any transition services.

(Authority: 20 U.S.C. 1414(d)(1)(B))

Note: The regular education teacher participating in a child's IEP meeting should be the teacher who is, or may be, responsible for implementing the IEP, so that the teacher can participate in discussions about how best to teach the child.

If the child has more than one teacher, the LEA may designate which teacher or teachers will participate. In a situation in which all of the child's teachers do not participate in the IEP meeting, the LEA is encouraged to seek input from teachers who will not be attending, and should ensure that any teacher not attending the meeting is informed about the results of the meeting (including receiving a copy of the IEP). In the case of a child whose behavior impedes the learning of the child or others, the LEA is encouraged to have a person knowledgeable about positive behavioral strategies at the IEP meeting.

Similarly, the special education teacher or provider participating in a child's IEP meeting should be the person who is, or will be, responsible for implementing the IEP. If, for example, the child's disability is a speech impairment, the teacher could be the speech-language pathologist.

Sec. 300.345 Parent participation.

(a)   Each public agency shall take steps to ensure that one or both of the parents of a child with a disability are present at each IEP meeting or are afforded the opportunity to participate, including—

   (1) Notifying parents of the meeting early enough to ensure that they will have an opportunity to attend; and

   (2) Scheduling the meeting at a mutually agreed on time and place.

(b) (1) The notice under paragraph (a)(1) of this section must indicate the purpose, time, and location of the meeting and who will be in attendance.

   (2) For a student with a disability beginning at age 14, or younger, if appropriate, the notice must also—

      (i) Indicate that a purpose of the meeting will be the development of a statement of the transition service needs of the student required in Sec. 300.347(b)(1)(i); and

      (ii) Indicate that the agency will invite the student.

   (3) For a student with a disability beginning at age 16, or younger, if appropriate, the notice must—

(i) Indicate that a purpose of the meeting is the consideration of needed transition services for the student required in Sec. 300.347(b)(1)(ii);

(ii) Indicate that the agency will invite the student; and

(iii) Identify any other agency that will be invited to send a representative.

(c) If neither parent can attend, the public agency shall use other methods to ensure parental participation, including individual or conference telephone calls.

(d) A meeting may be conducted without a parent in attendance if the public agency is unable to convince the parents that they should attend. In this case the public agency must have a record of its attempts to arrange a mutually agreed on time and place, such as—

(1) Detailed records of telephone calls made or attempted and the results of those calls;

(2) Copies of correspondence sent to the parents and any responses received; and

(3) Detailed records of visits made to the parent's home or place of employment and the results of those visits.

(e) The public agency shall take whatever action is necessary to ensure that the parent understands the proceedings at a meeting, including arranging for an interpreter for parents with deafness or whose native language is other than English.

(f) The public agency shall give the parent, on request, a copy of the IEP.

(Authority: 20 U.S.C. 1414(d)(1)(B)(i))

Note: The notice in paragraph (a) of this section could also inform parents that they may bring other people to the meeting consistent with Sec. 300.344(a)(6). As indicated in paragraph (d) of this section, the procedure used to notify parents (whether oral or written or both) is left to the discretion of the agency, but the agency must keep a record of its efforts to contact parents.

Sec. 300.346 Development, review, and revision of IEP.

(a) Development of IEP.

(1) General. In developing each child's IEP, the IEP team shall consider—

(i) The strengths of the child and the concerns of the parents for enhancing the education of their child; and

(ii) The results of the initial or most recent evaluation of the child.

(2) Consideration of special factors. The IEP team also shall—

(i) In the case of a child whose behavior impedes his or her learning or that of others, consider, if appropriate, strategies, including positive behavioral interventions, strategies, and supports to address that behavior;

(ii) In the case of a child with limited English proficiency, consider the language needs of the child as these needs relate to the child's IEP;

(iii) In the case of a child who is blind or visually impaired, provide for instruction in Braille and the use of Braille unless the IEP team determines, after an evaluation of the child's reading and writing skills, needs, and appropriate reading and writing media (including an evaluation of the child's future needs for instruction in Braille or the use of Braille), that instruction in Braille or the use of Braille is not appropriate for the child;

(iv) Consider the communication needs of the child, and in the case of a child who is deaf or hard of hearing, consider the child's language and communication needs, opportunities for direct communications with peers and professional personnel in the child's language and communication mode, academic level, and full range of needs, including opportunities for direct instruction in the child's language and communication mode; and

(v) Consider whether the child requires assistive technology devices and services.

(b) Review and Revision of IEP. In conducting a meeting to review, and, if appropriate, revise a child's IEP, the IEP team shall consider the factors described in paragraph (a) of this section.

(c) Statement in IEP. If, in considering the special factors described in paragraph (a)(1) and (2) of this section, the IEP team determines that a child needs a particular device or service (including an intervention, accommodation, or other program modification) in order for the child to receive FAPE, the IEP team must include a statement to that effect in the child's IEP.

(d) Requirement with respect to regular education teacher. The regular education teacher of a child with a disability, as a member of the IEP team, must, to the extent appropriate, participate in the development, review, and revision of the child's IEP, including assisting in—

   (1) The determination of appropriate positive behavioral interventions and strategies for the child; and

   (2) The determination of supplementary aids and services, program modifications, and supports for school personnel, consistent with Sec. 300.347(a)(3).

(e) Construction. Nothing in this section shall be construed to require the IEP team to include information under one component of a child's IEP that is already contained under another component of the child's IEP.

(Authority: 20 U.S.C. 1414 (d)(3) and (4)(B) and (e))

Note 1: The requirements of paragraph (a)(2) of this section (relating to consideration of special factors) were added by Pub.L. 105-17. These considerations are essential in assisting the IEP team to develop meaningful goals and other components of a child's IEP, if the considerations point to factors that could impede learning. The results of considering these special factors must, if appropriate, be reflected in the IEP goals, services, and provider responsibilities. As appropriate, consideration of these factors must include a review of valid evaluation data and the observed needs of the child resulting from the evaluation process.

Note 2: With respect to paragraph (a)(2)(iv) of this section (relating to special considerations for a child who is deaf or hard of hearing), the House Committee Report on Pub.L. 105-17 states that the IEP team should implement the provision in a manner consistent with the policy guidance entitled "Deaf Students Education Services," published in the Federal Register (57 FR 49274, October 30, 1992) by the Department (H. Rep. No. 105-95 (1997, p. 104)).

Note 3: In developing an IEP for a child with limited English proficiency (LEP), the IEP team must consider how the child's level of English language proficiency affects special education and related services that the child needs in order to receive FAPE. Under Title VI of the Civil Rights Act of 1964, school districts are required to provide LEP students with alternative language services to enable the student to acquire proficiency in English and to provide the student with meaningful access to the content of the educational curriculum that is available to all students, including special education and related services. An LEP student with a disability may require special education and related services for those aspects of the educational program which address the development of English language skills and other aspects of the student's educational program. For an LEP student with a disability, under paragraph (c) of this section, the IEP must address whether the special education and related services that the child needs will be provided in a language other than English.

Sec. 300.347 Content of IEP.

(a) General. The IEP for each child must include—

    (1) A statement of the child's present levels of educational performance, including—

        (i) How the child's disability affects the child's involvement and progress in the general curriculum; or

        (ii) For preschool children, as appropriate, how the disability affects the child's participation in appropriate activities;

    (2) A statement of measurable annual goals, including benchmarks or short-term objectives, related to—

        (i) Meeting the child's needs that result from the child's disability to enable the child to be involved in and progress in the general curriculum; and

        (ii) Meeting each of the child's other educational needs that result from the child's disability;

    (3) A statement of the special education and related services and supplementary aids and services to be provided to the child, or on behalf of the child, and a statement of the program modifications or supports for school personnel that will be provided for the child—

        (i) To advance appropriately toward attaining the annual goals;

(ii) To be involved and progress in the general curriculum in accordance with paragraph (a)(1) of this section and to participate in extracurricular and other nonacademic activities; and

(iii) To be educated and participate with other children with disabilities and nondisabled children in the activities described in this paragraph;

(4) An explanation of the extent, if any, to which the child will not participate with nondisabled children in the regular class and in the activities described in paragraph (a)(3) of this section;

(5) (i) A statement of any individual modifications in the administration of State- or district-wide assessments of student achievement that are needed in order for the child to participate in the assessment; and

(ii) If the IEP team determines that the child will not participate in a particular State- or district-wide assessment of student achievement (or part of an assessment), a statement of—

(A) Why that assessment is not appropriate for the child; and

(B) How the child will be assessed;

(6) The projected date for the beginning of the services and modifications described in paragraph (a)(3) of this section, and the anticipated frequency, location, and duration of those services and modifications; and

(7) A statement of—

(i) How the child's progress toward the annual goals described in paragraph (a)(2) of this section will be measured; and

(ii) How the child's parents will be regularly informed (through such means as periodic report cards), at least as often as parents are informed of their nondisabled children's progress, of—

(A) Their child's progress toward the annual goals; and

(B) The extent to which that progress is sufficient to enable the child to achieve the goals by the end of the year.

(b) Transition services.

(1) The IEP must include—

(i) For each student beginning at age 14 and younger, if appropriate, and updated annually, a statement of the transition service needs of the student under the applicable components of the student's IEP that focuses on the student's courses of study (such as participation in advanced-placement courses or a vocational education program); and

(ii) For each student beginning at age 16 (or younger, if determined appropriate by the IEP team), a statement of needed transition services for the student, including, if appropriate, a statement of the interagency responsibilities or any needed linkages.

(2) If the IEP team determines that services are not needed in one or more of the areas specified in Sec. 300.27(c)(1) through (c)(4), the IEP must include a statement to that effect and the basis upon which the determination was made.

(c) Transfer of rights. Beginning at least one year before a student reaches the age of majority under State law, the student's IEP must include a statement that the student has been informed of his or her rights under Part B of the Act, if any, that will transfer to the student on reaching the age of majority, consistent with Sec. 300.517.

(d) Students with disabilities convicted as adults and incarcerated in adult prisons. Special rules concerning the content of IEPs for students with disabilities convicted as adults and incarcerated in adult prisons are contained in Sec. 300.311(b) and (c).

(Authority: 20 U.S.C. 1414(d)(1)(A) and (d)(6)(A)(ii))

Note 1: Although the statute does not mandate transition services for all students below the age of 16, the provision of these services could have a significantly positive effect on the employment and independent living outcomes for many of these students in the future, especially for students who are likely to drop out before age 16.

Note 2: The IEP provisions added by Pub.L. 105-17 are intended to provide greater access by children with disabilities to the general curriculum and to educational reforms, as an effective means of ensuring better results for these children in preparing them for employment and independent living.

With respect to increased emphasis on the general curriculum, the House Committee Report on Pub.L. 105-17 includes the following statement:

> The Committee wishes to emphasize that, once a child has been identified as being eligible for special education, the connection between special education and related services and the child's opportunity to experience and benefit from the general education curriculum should be strengthened. The majority of children identified as eligible for special education and related services are capable of participating in the general education curriculum to varying degrees with some adaptations and modifications. This provision is intended to ensure that children's special education and related services are in addition to and are affected by the general education curriculum, not separate from it (H. Rep. No. 105-95 (1997, p. 99)).

Note 3: With respect to the impact on States and LEAs in implementing the new IEP provisions relating to accessing the general curriculum, the House Committee Report on Pub.L. 105-17 includes the following statement:

> The new emphasis on participation in the general education curriculum is not intended by the Committee to result in major expansions in the size of the IEP of dozens of pages of detailed goals and benchmarks or objectives in every curricular content standard skill. The new focus is intended to produce attention to the accommodations and adjustments necessary for disabled children to access the general education curriculum and the special services which may be necessary for the appropriate participation in particular areas of the curriculum due to the nature of the disability.

Note 4: With respect to paragraph (a) of this section, the House Committee Report on Pub.L. 105-17 includes the following statement:

> The Committee intends that, while teaching and related service methodologies or approaches are an appropriate topic for discussion and consideration by the IEP team during IEP development or annual review, they are not expected to be written into the IEP. Furthermore, the Committee does not intend that changing particular methods or approaches necessitates an additional meeting of the IEP team.
>
> Specific day to day adjustments in instructional methods and approaches that are made by either a regular or special education teacher to assist a disabled child to achieve his or her annual goals would not normally require action by the child's IEP team. However, if changes are contemplated in the child's measurable annual goals, benchmarks, or short-term objectives, or in any of the services or program modifications, or other components described in the child's IEP, the LEA must ensure that the child's IEP team is reconvened in a timely manner to address those changes (H. Rep. No. 105-95 (1997, pp. 100-101)).

Note 5: The provision in paragraph (a)(7)(ii) of this section concerning regularly informing parents of their child's progress toward annual goals and the extent to which this progress is sufficient to enable the child to achieve the goals by the end of the year is intended to be in addition to, rather than in place of, regular reporting to the parents (as for nondisabled children) of the child's progress in subjects or curricular areas for which the child is not receiving special education.

Note 6: With respect to paragraph (b)(1) of this section (relating to transition service needs beginning at age 14), the House Committee Report on Pub.L. 105-17 includes the following statement:

> The purpose of this requirement is to focus attention on how the child's educational program can be planned to help the child make a successful transition to his or her goals for life after secondary school. This provision is designed to augment, and not replace, the separate transition service requirement, under which children with disabilities beginning no later than age 16 receive transition services, including instruction, community experiences, the development of employment and other post-school objectives, and, when appropriate, independent living skills and functional vocational evaluation. For example, for a child whose transition goal is a job, a transition service could be teaching the child how to get to the job site on public transportation (H. Rep. No. 105-95 (1997, p. 101)).

Note 7: Each State must, at a minimum, ensure compliance with the transition service requirements in paragraph (b) of this section. However, it would not be a violation of this part for a public agency to begin planning for transition service needs and needed transition services for students younger than age 14 and age 16, respectively.

Sec. 300.348 Agency responsibilities for transition services.

(a) If a participating agency, other than the local educational agency, fails to provide the transition services described in the IEP in accordance with Sec. 300.347(b)(1)(ii), the local educational agency shall reconvene the IEP team to identify alternative strategies to meet the transition objectives for the child set out in the IEP.

(b) Nothing in this part relieves any participating agency, including a State vocational rehabilitation agency, of the responsibility to provide or pay for any transition service that the agency would otherwise provide to students with disabilities who meet the eligibility criteria of that agency.

(Authority: 20 U.S.C. 1414(d)(5); 1414(d)(1)(A)(vii))

Sec. 300.349 Private school placements by public agencies.

(a) Developing individualized education programs.

(1) Before a public agency places a child with a disability in, or refers a child to, a private school or facility, the agency shall initiate and conduct a meeting to develop an IEP for the child in accordance with Sec. 300.347.

(2) The agency shall ensure that a representative of the private school or facility attends the meeting. If the representative cannot attend, the agency shall use other methods to ensure participation by the private school or facility, including individual or conference telephone calls.

(b) Reviewing and revising individualized education programs.

(1) After a child with a disability enters a private school or facility, any meetings to review and revise the child's IEP may be initiated and conducted by the private school or facility at the discretion of the public agency.

(2) If the private school or facility initiates and conducts these meetings, the public agency shall ensure that the parents and an agency representative—

(i) Are involved in any decision about the child's IEP; and

(ii) Agree to any proposed changes in the program before those changes are implemented.

(c) Responsibility. Even if a private school or facility implements a child's IEP, responsibility for compliance with this part remains with the public agency and the SEA.

(Authority: 20 U.S.C. 1412(a)(10)(B))

Sec. 300.350 Children with disabilities in religiously-affiliated or other private schools.

If a child with a disability is enrolled in a religiously-affiliated or other private school and receives special education or related services from a public agency, the public agency shall—

(a) Initiate and conduct meetings to develop, review, and revise an IEP for the child, in accordance with Sec. 300.347; and

(b) Ensure that a representative of the religiously-affiliated or other private school attends each meeting. If the representative cannot attend, the agency shall use other methods to ensure participation by the private school, including individual or conference telephone calls.

(Authority. 20 U.S.C. 1112(a)(10)(A))

Sec. 300.351 Individualized education program—accountability.

Each public agency must provide special education and related services to a child with a disability in accordance with an IEP. However, Part B of the Act does not require that any agency, teacher, or other person be held accountable if a child does not achieve the growth projected in the annual goals and benchmarks or objectives.

(Authority: 20 U.S.C. 1414(d)); Cong. Rec. at H7152 (daily ed., July 21, 1975))

Note: This section is intended to relieve concerns that the IEP constitutes a guarantee by the public agency and the teacher that a child will progress at a specified rate. However, this section does not relieve agencies and teachers from making good faith efforts to assist the child in achieving the goals and objectives or benchmarks listed in the IEP. Part B is premised on children receiving the instruction, services, and modifications that they need to enable them to make progress in their education. Further, the section does not limit a parent's right to complain and ask for revisions of the child's IEP, or to invoke due process procedures (Sec. 300.507), if the parent feels that these efforts are not being made. This section does not prohibit a State or public agency from establishing its own accountability systems regarding teacher, school, or agency performance.

Appendix C—New and Old

In 1981, the U. S. Department of Education (DOE) added to the IDEA regulations Appendix C, which consisted largely of questions and answers interpreting the IEP requirements of the IDEA. In late 1997, the DOE issued a revised Appendix C, which incorporates the new requirements found in the IDEA Amendments of 1997. The 1981 Appendix offers school districts valuable guidance that is not included in the new version, and we present relevant selections here. We have omitted portions of both the 1998 and 1981 Appendix Cs that merely restate the text of the IDEA and offer no interpretation.

APPENDIX C TO PART 300 (1998, Abridged)

Interpretation of Individualized Education Program (IEP) Requirements of the Individuals with Disabilities Education Act (IDEA)

62 Federal Register 55123 (October 22, 1997) [Proposed Rules]

(Authority: Part B of the Education of the Handicapped Act, as amended (20 U.S.C. 1411-1420), unless otherwise noted.)

The IEP requirements of the IDEA emphasize the importance of each child with a disability's involvement and progress in the general curriculum; of the involvement of parents and students, together with regular and special education personnel, in making individualized decisions to support each child's educational success; and of preparing students with disabilities for employment and other post-school experiences. This Appendix provides guidance regarding Part B IEP requirements, especially as they relate to these core concepts, as well as other issues regarding the development and content of IEPs.

I. Involvement and Progress in the General Curriculum

In enacting the IDEA Amendments of 1997, the Congress found that:

… research, demonstration, and practice [over the past 20 years] in special education and related disciplines have demonstrated that an effective educational system now and in the future must—(A) maintain high academic standards and clear performance goals for children with disabilities, consistent with the standards and expectations for all students in the educational system, and provide for appropriate and effective strategies and methods to ensure that students who are children with disabilities have maximum opportunities to achieve those standards and goals. [Sec. 651(a)(6)(A) of the Act.]

Accordingly, the evaluation and IEP provisions of Part B place great emphasis on the involvement and progress of children with disabilities in the general curriculum. While the Act and regulations recognize that IEP teams must make individualized decisions about the special education and related services, and supplementary aids and services, provided to each child with a disability, they are driven by IDEA's strong preference that, to the maximum extent appropriate, children with disabilities be educated in regular classes with their nondisabled peers with appropriate supplementary aids and services.

2. *Must a child's IEP address his or her involvement in the general curriculum, regardless of the nature and severity of the child's disability and the setting in which the child is educated?*

    Yes. The IEP for all children with disabilities must address how the child will be involved and progress in the general curriculum, as described. The Part B regulations recognize that some children with disabilities will have some educational needs that result from their disabilities that cannot be fully met by involvement and progress in the general curriculum; accordingly, Sec. 300.347(a)(2) requires that each child's IEP include:

    A statement of measurable annual goals, including benchmarks or short-term objectives, related to—

(i) Meeting the child's needs that result from the child's disability to enable the child to be involved in and progress in the general curriculum; and

(ii) *meeting each of the child's other educational needs that result from the child's disability* [author's emphasis].

Thus, the IEP team for each child with a disability must make an individualized determination regarding how the child will participate in the general curriculum, and what, if any, educational needs that will not be met through involvement in the general curriculum should be addressed in the IEP. This includes children who are educated in separate classrooms or schools.

4. *Must the measurable annual goals in a child's IEP address all areas of the general curriculum, or only those areas in which the child's involvement and progress are affected by the child's disability?*

Section 300.347(a)(2) requires that each child's IEP include a "… statement of measurable annual goals, including benchmarks or short-term objectives, related to—(i) Meeting the child's needs that result from the child's disability to enable the child to be involved in and progress in the general curriculum; and (ii) meeting each of the child's other educational needs that result from the child's disability …." Thus, a public agency is not required to include in an IEP annuals goals that relate to areas of the general curriculum in which the child's disability does not affect the child's ability to be involved in and progress in the general curriculum.

II. Involvement of Parents and Students

One of the key purposes of the IDEA Amendments of 1997 is to "… expand and promote opportunities for parents, special education, related services, regular education, and early intervention service providers, and other personnel to work in new partnerships at both the State and local levels" (House Report 105-95 (1997, p. 82)). Indeed, the Committee viewed the Amendments as an opportunity to "[strengthen] the role of parents" (House Report 105-95 (1997, p. 82)). Accordingly, the Amendments require that parents have "… an opportunity … to participate in meetings with respect to the identification, evaluation, and educational placement of the child, and the provision of FAPE to the child" (Sec. 300.501). Parents must now be part of the teams that determine what additional data are needed as part of an evaluation of their child (Sec. 300.533(a)(1)); their child's eligibility (Sec. 300.534(a)(1)); and the educational placement of their child (Sec. 300.501(c)). Parents' concerns, and information that they provide regarding their children, must be considered in developing and reviewing their children's IEPs (Secs. 300.343(c)(iii) and 300.346 (a)(1)(i) and (b)).

As explained, the requirements for keeping parents informed about the educational progress of their children, particularly as it relates to their progress in the general curriculum, have been strengthened (Sec. 300.347(a)(7)).

The IDEA Amendments of 1997 and the 1990 Amendments have both included provisions which greatly strengthen involvement of students with disabilities in decisions regarding their own futures, to facilitate movement from school to post-school activities. The IDEA Amendments of 1990 included provisions regarding transition services, which require: (a) a coordinated set of activities within an outcome-oriented process to facilitate movement from school to post-school activities; (b) that the transition services provided to each student be "… based on the individual student's needs, taking into account the student's preferences and interests" (Sec. 300.27(b)); (c) that the public agency invite a student with a disability to any IEP meetings for which a purpose is the consideration of transition services (Sec. 300.344(b)(1)), and that, if "… the student does not attend, the public agency … take other steps to ensure that the student's preferences and interests are considered (Sec. 300.344(b)(2)). States may now transfer most parental rights under Part B to the student when the student reaches the age of majority under State law (Sec. 300.517), and beginning at least one year before a student reaches the age of majority under State law, the IEP must include a statement that the student has been informed of any rights that will transfer to him or her upon reaching the age of majority (Sec. 300.347(c)).

5. *What is the role of the parents, including surrogate parents, in decisions regarding the educational program of their children?*

    The parents of a child with a disability are expected to be equal participants along with school personnel, in developing, reviewing, and revising the IEP for their child. This is an active role in which the parents: (1) provide critical information about their child's abilities, interests, performance, and history, (2) participate in the discussion about the child's need for special education and related services and supplementary aids and services, and (3) join with the other participants in deciding how the child will be involved and progress in the general curriculum and participate in State- and district-wide assessments, and what services the agency will provide to the child and in what setting. As noted, Part B specifically provides that parents have the right to:

(a) Participate in meetings about their child's identification, evaluation, educational program (including IEP meetings), and educational placement (Secs. 300.344(a)(1) and 300.517);

(b) Be part of the teams that determine what additional data are needed as part of an evaluation of their child (Sec. 300.533(a)(1)), and determine their child's eligibility (Sec. 300.534(a)(1)) and educational placement (Sec. 300.501(c));

(c) Have their concerns and information that they provide regarding their child considered in developing and reviewing their child's IEPs (Secs. 300.343(c)(iii) and 300.346 (a)(1)(i) and (b)); and

(d) Be regularly informed (by such means as periodic report cards), as specified in their child's IEP, at least as often as parents are informed of their nondisabled children's progress, of their child's progress toward the annual goals in the IEP and the extent to which that progress is sufficient to enable the child to achieve the goals by the end of the year (Sec. 300.347(a)(7)). A surrogate parent is a person appointed to represent the interests of a child with a disability in the educational decision-making process when no parent (as defined at Sec. 300.19) is known, the agency, after reasonable efforts, cannot locate the child's parents, or the child is a ward of the State under the laws of the State. A surrogate parent has all of the rights and responsibilities of a parent under Part B. Thus, the surrogate parent is entitled to: (1) participate in the child's IEP meeting, (2) examine the child's education records, and (3) receive notice, grant consent, and invoke due process to resolve differences. (See Sec. 300.515, Surrogate parents.)

6. *What are the Part B requirements regarding the participation of a child or youth with a disability in an IEP meeting?*

If a purpose of an IEP meeting will be the consideration of needed transition services, the public agency must invite the student and, as part of notification to the parent of the IEP meeting, inform the parents that the agency will invite the student to the IEP meeting. If the student does not attend, the public agency must take other steps to ensure that the student's preferences and interests are considered. Section Sec. 300.517 permits States to transfer procedural rights under Part B from the parents to students with disabilities who reach the age of majority under State law, but who have not been determined to be incompetent under State law. If procedural rights under Part B are, consistent with State law and Sec. 300.517, transferred from the parents to the student, the public agency would be required to ensure that the student has the right to participate in IEP meetings set forth for parents in Sec. 300.345. However, at the discretion of the student or the public agency, the parents also could attend IEP meetings as "... individuals who have knowledge or special expertise regarding the child ..." (see Sec. 300.344(a)(6)).

In other circumstances, the child may attend "if appropriate" (Sec. 300.344(a)(7)). Generally, a child with a disability should attend the IEP meeting if the parent decides that it is appropriate for the child to do so. If possible, the agency and parents should discuss the appropriateness of the child's participation before a decision is made, in order to help the parents determine whether or not the child's attendance will be: (1) helpful in developing the IEP, or (2) directly beneficial to the child or both. The agency should inform the parents before each IEP meeting—as part of notification under Sec. 300.345(a)(1)—that they may invite their child to participate.

7. *Must the public agency let the parents know who will be at the IEP meeting?*

   Yes. In notifying parents about the meeting, the agency "... must indicate the purpose, time, and location of the meeting, and who will be in attendance" (Sec. 300.345(b)). In addition, if a purpose of the IEP meeting is the consideration of transition services for a student, the notice must also inform the parents that the agency is inviting the student, and identify any other agency that will be invited to send a representative. The public agency should also inform the parents of their right to invite to the meeting "... other individuals who have knowledge or special expertise regarding the child, including related services personnel as appropriate ..." (Sec. 300.344(a)(6)). It is also appropriate for the agency to ask the parents what if any individuals they will to bring to the meeting.

8. Do parents have the right to a copy of their child's IEP?

Yes. Section 300.345(f) states that the public agency shall give the parent, on request, a copy of the IEP. It is recommended that public agencies provide parents with a copy of the IEP within a reasonable time following the IEP meeting, or inform them at the IEP meeting of their right to request and receive a copy.

9. What is a public agency's responsibility if it is not possible to reach consensus on what services should be included in a child's IEP?

The IEP meeting serves as a communication vehicle between parents and school personnel, and enables them, as equal participants, to make joint, informed decisions regarding the child's needs and appropriate goals, the extent to which the child will be involved in the general curriculum and participate in the regular education environment and State- and district-wide assessments, and the services needed to support that involvement and participation and to achieve agreed-upon goals. Parents are to be equal partners with school personnel in making these decisions, and the IEP team must consider parents' concerns and information that they provide regarding their child in developing and reviewing IEPs (Secs. 300.343(c)(iii) and 300.346(a)(1) and (b)).

The IEP team should work toward consensus, but the public agency has ultimate responsibility to ensure that the IEP includes the services that the child needs in order to receive FAPE. If it is not possible to reach consensus in an IEP meeting, the public agency must provide the parents with prior written notice of the agency's proposals or refusals, or both, regarding the child's educational program and placement, and the parents have the right to seek resolution of any disagreements through mediation or other informal means, or by initiating an impartial due process hearing. Every effort should be made to resolve differences between parents and school staff through voluntary mediation or some other informal step, without resort to a due process hearing. However, mediation or other informal procedures may not be used to deny or delay a parent's right to a due process hearing.

10. *Does Part B require that public agencies inform parents regarding the educational progress of their children with disabilities?*

Yes, the Part B statute and regulations include a number of provisions to help ensure that parents are involved in decisions regarding, and informed about, their child's educational progress, including the child's progress in the general curriculum. First, the parents will be informed regarding their child's present levels of educational performance through the development of the IEP. Section 300.347(a)(1) requires that each IEP include:

> ... a statement of the child's present levels of educational performance, including—(i) How the child's disability affects the child's involvement and progress in the general curriculum; or (ii) for preschool children, as appropriate, how the disability affects the child's participation in appropriate activities ....

Further, Sec. 300.347(a)(7) sets forth requirements for regularly informing parents about their child's educational progress. That section requires that the IEP include:

> ... a statement of—(i) How the child's progress toward the annual goals ... will be measured; and (ii) how the child's parents will be regularly informed (by such means as periodic report cards), at least as often as parents of nondisabled children are informed, of—(A) their child's progress toward the annual goals ... ; and (B) the extent to which that progress is sufficient to enable the child to achieve the goals by the end of the year.

Finally, the parents will, as part of the IEP team, participate, at least once every 12 months, in a review of their child's educational progress. Part B requires that a public agency initiate and conduct a meeting, at which the IEP team:

> ... (1) Reviews the child's IEP periodically, but not less than annually to determine whether the annual goals for the child are being achieved; and (2) revises the IEP as appropriate to address—(i) any lack of expected progress toward the annual goals ... and in the general curriculum, if appropriate; (ii) the results of any reevaluation ... ; (iii) information about the child provided to, or by, the parents ... ; (iv) the child's anticipated needs; or (v) other matters.

IV. Other Questions Regarding the Development and Content of IEPs

14. For a child with a disability receiving special education for the first time, when must an IEP be developed—before placement or after placement?

Section 300.342(b)(1) requires that an IEP be "… in effect before special education and related services are provided to a child." The appropriate placement for a particular child with a disability cannot be determined until after decisions have been made about the child's needs and the services that the public agency will provide to meet those needs. These decisions must be made at the IEP meeting, and it would not be permissible first to place the child and then develop the IEP. Therefore, the IEP must be developed before placement. This requirement does not preclude temporarily placing an eligible child with a disability in a program as part of the evaluation process—before the IEP is finalized—to assist a public agency in determining the appropriate placement for the child. It is essential that the temporary placement not become the final placement before the IEP is finalized. In order to ensure that this does not happen, the State might consider requiring LEAs to take the following actions:

a. Develop an interim IEP for the child that sets out the specific conditions and timelines for the trial placement. (See paragraph c.)

b. Ensure that the parents agree to the interim placement before it is carried out, and that they are involved throughout the process of developing, reviewing, and revising the child's IEP.

c. Set a specific timeline (e.g., 30 days) for completing the evaluation, finalizing the IEP, and making judgments about the most appropriate placement for the child.

d. Conduct an IEP meeting at the end of the trial period in order to finalize the child's IEP.

15. *Who is responsible for ensuring the development of IEPs for children*
     with disabilities served by a public agency other than an LEA?

The answer as to which public agency has direct responsibility for ensuring
the development of IEPs for children with disabilities served by a public
agency other than an LEA will vary from State to State, depending upon
State law, policy, or practice. The SEA is ultimately responsible for ensuring
that all Part B requirements, including the IEP requirements, are met for eligible children within the State, including those children served by a public
agency other than an LEA. (See Sec. 300.600 regarding the SEA's general su-
pervisory responsibility for all education programs for children with disabilities, with one exception. The Governor [or another individual pursuant to
State law] may, consistent with State law, assign to any public agency in the
State the responsibility of ensuring that Part B requirements are met with respect to children with disabilities who are convicted as adults under State law
and incarcerated in adult prisons.)

The SEA must ensure that every child with a disability in the State has FAPE
available, regardless of which State or local agency is responsible for educating the child. (The only exception to this responsibility is that, as noted, the
SEA is not responsible for ensuring that FAPE is made available to children
with disabilities who are convicted as adults under State law and incarcerated in adult prisons, if the State has assigned that responsibility to a public
agency other than the SEA.) Although the SEA has flexibility in deciding the
best means to meet this obligation (e.g., through interagency agreements),
the SEA must ensure that no eligible child with a disability is denied FAPE
due to jurisdictional disputes among agencies.

When an LEA is responsible for the education of a child with a disability, the
LEA remains responsible for developing the child's IEP, regardless of the public or private school setting into which it places the child.

16. *For a child placed out of State by an educational or noneducational*
     State or local agency, is the placing or receiving State responsible for
     the child's IEP?

Regardless of the reason for the placement, the "placing" State is responsible
for developing the child's IEP and ensuring that it is implemented. The determination of the specific agency in the placing State that is responsible for the

child's IEP would be based on State law, policy, or practice. However, the SEA in the placing State is responsible for ensuring that the child has FAPE available.

17. *If a disabled child has been receiving special education from one public agency and transfers to another public agency in the same State, must the new public agency develop an IEP before the child can be placed in a special education program?*

If a child with a disability changes school districts in the same State, the State and its public agencies have an ongoing responsibility to ensure that the child receives FAPE, and the new public agency is responsible for ensuring that the child receives special education and related services in conformity with an IEP. The new public agency must ensure that the child has an IEP in effect before the agency can provide special education and related services. The new public agency may meet this responsibility by either adopting the IEP the former public agency developed for the child or by developing a new IEP for the child. Before the child's IEP is finalized, the new public agency may provide interim services agreed upon by both the parents and the new public agency. If the parents and the new public agency are unable to agree on an interim IEP and placement, the new public agency must implement the old IEP to the extent possible until a new IEP is developed and implemented. In general, while the new public agency must conduct an IEP meeting, it would not be necessary if: (1) a copy of the child's current IEP is available; (2) the parents indicate that they are satisfied with the current IEP; and (3) the new public agency determines that the current IEP is appropriate and can be implemented as written.

If the child's current IEP is not available, or if either the new public agency or the parent believes that it is not appropriate, the new public agency must conduct an IEP meeting within a short time after the child enrolls in the new public agency (normally, within one week).

18. *What timelines apply to the development and implementation of an initial IEP for a child with a disability?*

Section 300.343(b) requires a public agency to: (1) ensure that an offer of services in accordance with an IEP is made to parents within a reasonable period of time from the agency's receipt of parental consent to an initial evaluation; and (2) in meeting that timeline, conduct a meeting to develop the IEP within 30 calendar days of a determination that the child needs special education and related services. Section 300.342(b)(2) requires that an IEP be implemented as soon as possible following the meeting in which the IEP is developed.

19. *Must a public agency hold separate meetings to determine a child's eligibility for special education and related services, develop the child's IEP, and determine the child's placement, or may the agency meet all of these requirements in a single meeting?*

A public agency may, after a child is determined by "a team of qualified professionals and the parent" (see Sec. 300.534(a)(1)) to be a child with a disability who needs special education services, continue in the same meeting to develop an IEP for the child and to determine the child's placement. However, the public agency must ensure that it: (1) meets all of the Part B requirements regarding meetings to develop IEPs, including providing appropriate notification to the parents, consistent with the requirements of Sec. 300.345, and including the required team participants, consistent with the requirements of Sec. 300.344; and (2) the requirements of Sec. 300.533 regarding eligibility decisions.

20. *How frequently must a public agency conduct meetings to review, and if appropriate revise, the IEP for each child with a disability?*

A public agency must initiate and conduct meetings periodically, but at least once every 12 months, to determine whether the annual goals for the child are being achieved, and to revise the IEP as appropriate to address: (a) any lack of expected progress toward the annual goals and in the general curriculum, if appropriate; (b) the results of any reevaluation; (c) information about the child provided to, or by, the parents; (d) the child's anticipated needs; or (e) other matters (Sec. 300.343(c)).

A public agency must also ensure that an IEP is in effect for each child at the beginning of each school year (Sec. 300.342(a)). It may conduct IEP meetings at any time during the year. However, if the agency conducts the IEP meeting prior to the beginning of the next school year, it must ensure that the IEP contains the necessary special education and related services and supplementary aids and services to ensure that the student's IEP can be appropriately implemented during the next school year. Otherwise, it would be necessary for the public agency to conduct another IEP meeting. Although the public agency is responsible for determining when it is necessary to conduct an IEP meeting, the parents of a child with a disability have the right to request an IEP meeting at any time. For example, if the parents believe that the child is not progressing satisfactorily or that there is a problem with the child's current IEP, it would be appropriate for the parents to request an IEP meeting. If a child's teachers feels that the child's placement or IEP services are not appropriate to the child, the teacher should follow agency procedures with respect to: (1) calling or meeting with the parents, or (2) requesting the agency to hold another IEP meeting to review the child's IEP. The legislative history of Public Law 94-142 makes it clear that there should be as many meetings a year as any one child may need (121 Cong. Rec. S20428-29 (Nov. 19, 1975) (remarks of Senator Stafford)).

In general, if either a parent or a public agency believes that a required component of the student's IEP should be changed, the public agency must conduct an IEP meeting if it believes that the question of whether the student's IEP needs to be revised to ensure the provision of FAPE to the student is a matter that must be considered by the IEP team. If a parent requests an IEP meeting because the parent believes that a change in the provision of FAPE to the child or the educational placement of the child, and the agency refuses to convene an IEP meeting to determine whether such a change is needed, the agency must provide written notice to the parents of the refusal, including an explanation of why the agency has determined that conducting the meeting is not necessary to ensure the provision of FAPE to the student. Under Sec. 300.506(a), the parents or agency may initiate a due process hearing at any time regarding any proposal or refusal regarding the identification, evaluation, or educational placement of the child, or the provision of FAPE to the child.

22. *Who can serve as the representative of the public agency at an IEP meeting?*

The IEP team must include a representative of the local educational agency who: (a) is qualified to provide, or supervise the provision of, specially designed instruction to meet the unique needs of children with disabilities; (b) is knowledgeable about the general curriculum; and (c) is knowledgeable about the availability of resources of the local educational agency

(Sec. 300.344(a)(4)). Each State or local agency may determine which specific staff member will serve as the agency representative in a particular IEP meeting, so long as the individual meets these requirements. It is, however, important that the agency representative have the authority to commit agency resources and be able to ensure that whatever services are set out in the IEP will actually be provided.

Note: IEP meetings for continuing placements may in some instances be more routine than those for initial placements, and, thus, may not require the participation of a key administrator.

23. *For a child with a disability being considered for initial placement in special education, which teacher or teachers should attend the IEP meeting?*

A child's IEP team must include at least one of the student's regular education teachers (if the child is, or may be, participating in the regular education environment) and at least one special education teacher, or, if appropriate, at least one of the child's special education providers (Sec. 300.344(a)(2) and (3)). Each IEP must include a statement of present levels of educational performance, including a statement of how the child's disability affects the child's involvement and progress in the general curriculum (Sec. 300.347(a)(1)). The regular education teacher is a required participant on the IEP team of a child who is, or may be, participating in the regular educational environment, regardless of the extent of that participation.

The child's special education teacher could be either: (1) a teacher qualified to provide special education in the child's area of suspected disability, or (2) another special education provider such as a speech pathologist, physical or occupational therapist, etc., if the related service consists of specially designed instruction and is considered special education under the applicable State standard.

Note: Sometimes more than one meeting is necessary in order to finalize a child's IEP. In this process, if the special education teacher who will be working with the child is identified, it would be useful to have that teacher participate in the meeting with the parents and other members of the IEP team in finalizing the IEP. If this is not possible, the agency should ensure that the teacher is given a copy of the child's IEP as soon as possible after the IEP is finalized and before the teacher begins working with the child.

24. *If a child with a disability attends several regular classes, must all of the child's regular education teachers attend the IEP meeting?*

No. The IEP team need not include more than one regular education teacher of the child. If the participation of more than one regular education teacher is considered by the agency or the parents to be beneficial to the child's success in school (e.g., in terms of enhancing the child's participation in the general curriculum), it would be appropriate for them to attend the meeting.

25. *For a child whose primary disability is a speech impairment, may a public agency meet its responsibility under Sec. 300.344(a)(3) to ensure that the IEP team includes "… at least one special education teacher, or, if appropriate, at least one special education provider of the child" by including a speech-language pathologist in the IEP team?*

Yes, if speech is considered special education under State standards. As with other children with disabilities, the IEP team must also include at least one of the child's regular education teachers if the child is, or may be, participating in the regular education environment.

26. *Do public agencies and parents have the option of bringing any individual of their choice to a student's IEP meeting? Would it be permissible for other individuals to attend IEP meetings at the discretion of the parents or the agency?*

The IEP team may, at the discretion of the parent or the agency, include "… other individuals who have knowledge or special expertise regarding the child …" (Sec. 300.344(a)(6)). This is a change from prior law, which had provided, without qualification, that parents or agencies could bring other individuals to IEP meetings at the discretion of the parents or agency. However, the legislative history of Public Law 94-142 made it clear that attendance at IEP meetings should be limited to those who have an intense interest in the child (121 Cong. Rec. S10974 (June 18, 1975) (remarks of Senator Randolph)).

Part B does not provide for the participation of individuals such as representatives of teacher organizations or attorneys at IEP meetings. For example, since a representative of a teacher organization would be concerned with the interests of the teacher rather than the interests of the child, and generally would not possess knowledge or expertise regarding the child, it generally would be inappropriate for such an official to attend an IEP meeting. While either the parent or public agency may consider inviting their attorneys to an IEP meeting, parents and public agencies need to ensure that their attorneys possess knowledge and expertise regarding the child to warrant their participation. However, the participation of attorneys at IEP meetings should be discouraged if their participation would have the potential for creating an adversarial atmosphere which would not necessarily be in the best interests of the child. Further, as provided in Section 615(i)(3)(D)(ii) of the Act, attorneys' fees may not be awarded relating to any meeting of the IEP team unless such meeting is convened as a result of an administrative proceeding or judicial action, or, at the discretion of the State, for a mediation "… conducted prior to the [request for a due process hearing]."

27. *Must related service personnel attend IEP meetings?*

Although Part B does not expressly require that the IEP team include related service personnel as part of the IEP team (Sec. 300.344(a)), it is appropriate for those persons to be included if a particular related service is to be discussed as part of the IEP meeting. Section 300.344(a)(6) provides that the IEP team also includes "… at the discretion of the parent or the agency, other individuals who have knowledge or special expertise regarding the child, including related services personnel as appropriate …."

Further, Sec. 300.344(a)(3) requires that the IEP team for each child with a disability include "… at least one special education teacher, or, if appropriate, at least one special education provider of the child …." This requirement can be met by the participation of either: (1) a special education teacher of the child, or (2) another special education provider such as a speech pathologist, physical or occupational therapist, etc., if the related service consists of specially designed instruction and is considered special education under the applicable State standard. If a child with a disability has an identified need for related services, it would be appropriate for the related service personnel to attend the meeting or otherwise be involved in developing the IEP. As explained in the House Report on the IDEA Amendments of 1997, "Related service personnel should be included on the team when a particular related service will be discussed at the request of the child's parents or the school" (House Report 105-95 (1997, p. 103)). For example, if the child's evaluation indicates the need for a specific related service (e.g., physical therapy, occupational therapy, special transportation services, school social work services, school health services, or counseling), the agency should ensure that a qualified provider of that service either: (1) attends the IEP meeting, or (2) provides a written recommendation concerning the nature, frequency, and amount of service to be provided to the child. This written recommendation could be a part of the evaluation report.

28. *Must the public agency ensure that all services specified in a child's IEP are provided?*

Yes. The public agency must ensure that all services set forth in the child's IEP are provided, consistent with the child's needs as identified in the IEP. It may provide each of those services directly, through its own staff resources; indirectly, by contracting with another public or private agency; or through other arrangements. In providing the services, the agency may use whatever State, local, Federal, and private sources of support are available for those purposes (see Sec. 300.301(a)), but the services must be at no cost to the parents, and the public agency remains responsible for ensuring that the IEP services are provided in a manner that appropriately meets the student's needs as specified in the IEP. The SEA and responsible public agency may not allow the failure of another agency to provide services described in the child's IEP to deny or delay the provision of FAPE to a child.

29. *Is it permissible for an agency to have the IEP completed before the IEP meeting begins?*

No. Agency staff may come to an IEP meeting prepared with evaluation findings and proposed recommendations regarding IEP content, but the agency must make it clear to the parents at the outset of the meeting that the services proposed by the agency are only recommendations for review and discussion with the parents. Agencies that use this approach must ensure that there is a full discussion with the parents of the child's needs and the services to be provided to meet those needs before the child's IEP is finalized.

30. *Must a public agency include transportation in a child's IEP as a related service?*

A public agency must provide transportation as a related service if it is required to assist the disabled child to benefit from special education. (This includes transporting a preschool-aged child to the site at which the public agency provides special education and related services to the child, if that site is different from the site at which the child receives other preschool or day-care services.) In determining whether to include transportation in a child's IEP, the IEP team must consider how the child's disability affects the child's need for transportation, including determining whether the child's disability prevents the child from using the same transportation provided to nondisabled children, or from getting to school in the same manner as nondisabled children. The public agency must ensure that any transportation service included in a child's IEP as a related service is provided at public expense and at no cost to the parents, and that the child's IEP describes the transportation arrangement.

Even if a child's IEP team determines that the child does not require transportation as a related service, Section 504 of the Rehabilitation Act of 1973 requires that the child receive the same transportation provided to nondisabled children. If a public agency transports nondisabled children, it must transport disabled children under the same terms and conditions. However, if a child's IEP team determines that a student does not need transportation as a related service, and the public agency transports only those children whose IEPs specify transportation as a related service, and does not transport nondisabled children, the public agency would not be required to provide transportation to a disabled child.

31. *Must a public agency provide related services that are required to assist a child with a disability to benefit from special education, whether or not those services are included in the list of related services in Sec. 300.16?*

The Note following Sec. 300.16 clarifies that "... [T]he list of related services is not exhaustive and may include other developmental, corrective, or supportive services ... if they are required to assist a child with a disability to benefit from special education." This could, depending upon the unique needs of a child, include such services as nutritional services or service coordination.

32. *Must the IEP specify the amount of services or may it simply list the services to be provided?*

The amount of services to be provided must be stated in the IEP, so that the level of the agency's commitment of resources will be clear to the parents and other IEP team members. The amount of time to be committed to each of the various services to be provided must be: (1) appropriate to the specific service, and (2) stated in the IEP in a manner that is clear to all who are involved in both the development and implementation of the IEP.

Appendix C to Part 300 (1981, Abridged)

Interpretation of Individualized Education Program (IEP) Requirements
of the Individuals with Disabilities Education Act (IDEA)

46 Federal Register 5461 (January 19, 1981)
34 CFR Part 300

(Authority: Part B of the Education of the Handicapped Act, as amended (20 U.S.C. 1411-1420), unless otherwise noted.)

There are two main parts of the IEP requirement, as described in the Act and regulations: (1) the IEP meeting(s), at which parents and school personnel jointly make decisions about a handicapped child's educational program, and (2) the IEP document itself, which is a written record of the decisions reached at the meeting. The overall IEP requirement, comprised of these two parts, has a number of purposes and functions:

> a. The IEP meeting serves as a communication vehicle between parents and school personnel, and enables them, as equal participants, to jointly decide what the child's needs are, what services will be provided to meet those needs, and what the anticipated outcomes may be.

> b. The IEP process provides an opportunity for resolving any differences between the parents and the agency concerning a handicapped child's special education needs; first, through the IEP meeting, and second, if necessary, through the procedural protections that are available to the parents.

> c. The IEP sets forth in writing a commitment of resources necessary to enable a handicapped child to receive needed special education and related services.

> d. The IEP is a management tool that is used to ensure that each handicapped child is provided special education and related services appropriate to the child's special learning needs.

> e. The IEP is a compliance/monitoring document which may be used by authorized monitoring personnel from each governmental level to determine whether a handicapped child is actually receiving the free appropriate public education agreed to by the parents and the school.

f. The IEP serves as an evaluation device for use in determining the extent of the child's progress toward meeting the projected outcomes.

Note: The Act does not require that teachers or other school personnel be held accountable if a handicapped child does not achieve the goals and objectives set forth in the IEP. See Sec. 300.349, Individualized education program—accountability.

20. *When may representatives of teacher organizations attend IEP meetings?*

Under the Family Educational Rights and Privacy Act (FERPA; 20 U.S.C. 1232g) and implementing regulations (34 CFR Part 99), officials of teacher organizations may not attend IEP meetings at which personally identifiable information from the student's education records may be discussed except with the prior written consent of the parents. (See 34 CFR 99.30(a)(1).)

In addition, EHA-B does not provide for the participation of representatives of teacher organizations at IEP meetings. The legislative history of the Act makes it clear that attendance at IEP meetings should be limited to those who have an intense interest in the child (121 Cong. Rec. S10974 (June 18, 1975) (remarks of Senator Randolph)). Since a representative of a teacher organization would be concerned with the interests of the teacher rather than the interests of the child, it would be inappropriate for such an official to attend an IEP meeting.

24. *Are agencies required to use a case manager in the development of a handicapped child's IEP?*

No. However, some agencies have found it helpful to have a special educator or some other school staff member (e.g., a social worker, counselor, or psychologist) serve as coordinator or case manager of the IEP process for an individual child or for all handicapped children served by the agency. Examples of the kinds of activities which case managers might carry out are: (1) coordinating the multidisciplinary evaluation; (2) collecting and synthesizing the evaluation reports and other relevant information about a child that might be needed at the IEP meeting; (3) communicating with the parents; and (4) participating in, or conducting, the IEP meeting itself.

36. *What should be included in the statement of the child's present levels of educational performance?*

The statement of present levels of educational performance will be different for each handicapped child. Thus, determinations about the content of the statement for an individual child are matters that are left to the discretion of participants in the IEP meetings. However, the following are some points which should be taken into account in writing this part of the IEP.

a. The statement should accurately describe the effect of the child's handicap on the child's performance in any area of education that is affected, including: (1) academic areas (e.g., reading, math, communication, etc.), and (2) nonacademic areas (e.g., daily life activities, mobility, etc.).

Note: Labels such as "mentally retarded" or "deaf" may not be used as a substitute for the description of present levels of educational performance.

b. The statement should be written in objective measurable terms, to the extent possible. Data from the child's evaluation would be a good source of such information. Test scores that are pertinent to the child's diagnosis might be included, where appropriate. However, the scores should be: (1) self-explanatory (i.e., they can be interpreted by all participants without the use of test manuals or other aids), or (2) an explanation should be included. Whatever test results are used should reflect the impact of the handicap on the child's performance. Thus, raw scores would not usually be sufficient.

c. There should be a direct relationship between the present levels of educational performance and the other components of the IEP. Thus, if the statement describes a problem with the child's reading level and points to a deficiency in a specific reading skill, this problem should be addressed under both: (1) goals and objectives, and (2) specific special education and related services to be provided to the child.

37. *Why are goals and objectives required in the IEP?*

The statutory requirements for including annual goals and short-term objectives (Section 602(19)(B)), and for having at least an annual review of a handicapped child's IEP (Section 614(a)(5)), provide a mechanism for determining:

(1) whether the anticipated outcomes for the child are being met (i.e., whether the child is progressing in the special education program), and (2) whether the placement and services are appropriate to the child's special learning needs. In effect, these requirements provide a way for the child's teacher(s) and parents to be able to track the child's progress in special education. However, the goals and objectives in the IEP are not intended to be as specific as the goals and objectives that are normally found in daily, weekly, or monthly instructional plans.

38. What are "annual goals" in an IEP?

The annual goals in the IEP are statements which describe what a handicapped child can reasonably be expected to accomplish within a 12-month period in the child's special education program. As indicated under Question 36, above, there should be a direct relationship between the annual goals and the present levels of educational performance.

39. What are "short-term instructional objectives" in an IEP?

Short-term instructional objectives (also called "IEP objectives") are measurable, intermediate steps between a handicapped child's present levels of educational performance and the annual goals that are established for the child. The objectives are developed based upon a logical breakdown of the major components of the annual goals, and can serve as milestones for measuring progress toward meeting the goals.

In some respects, IEP objectives are similar to objectives used in daily classroom instructional plans. For example, both kinds of objectives are used: (1) to describe what a given child is expected to accomplish in a particular area within some specified time period, and (2) to determine the extent to which the child is progressing toward those accomplishments.

In other respects, objectives in IEPs are different from those used in instructional plans, primarily in the amount of detail they provide. IEP objectives provide general benchmarks for determining progress toward meeting the annual goals. These objectives should be projected to be accomplished over an extended period of time (e.g., an entire school quarter or semester). On the other hand, the objectives in classroom instructional plans deal with more specific outcomes that are to be accomplished on a daily, weekly, or monthly

basis. Classroom instructional plans generally include details not required in
an IEP, such as the specific methods, activities, and materials (e.g., use of
flash cards) that will be used in accomplishing the objectives.

40. *Should the IEP goals and objectives focus only on special education
    and related services, or should they relate to the total education of
    the child?*

IEP goals and objectives are concerned primarily with meeting a handicapped child's need for special education and related services, and are not required to cover other areas of the child's education. Stated another way, the
goals and objectives in the IEP should focus on offsetting or reducing the
problems resulting from the child's handicap which interfere with learning
and educational performance in school. For example, if a learning disabled
child is functioning several grades below the child's indicated ability in reading and has a specific problem with word recognition, the IEP goals and objectives would be directed toward: (1) closing the gap between the child's
indicated ability and current level of functioning, and (2) helping the child increase the ability to use word attack skills effectively (or to find some other
approach to increase independence in reading).

For a child with a mild speech impairment, the IEP objectives would focus
on improving the child's communication skills, by either: (1) correcting the
impairment, or (2) minimizing its effect on the child's ability to communicate. On the other hand, the goals and objectives for a severely retarded child
would be more comprehensive and cover more of the child's school program
than if the child has only a mild handicap.

41. *Should there be a relationship between the goals and objectives in the
    IEP and those that are in instructional plans of special education
    personnel?*

Yes. There should be a direct relationship between the IEP goals and objectives for a given handicapped child and the goals and objectives that are in
the special education instructional plans for the child. However, the IEP is
not intended to be detailed enough to be used as an instructional plan. The
IEP, through its goals and objectives: (1) sets the general direction to be
taken by those who will implement the IEP, and (2) serves as the basis for
developing a detailed instructional plan for the child.

44. *Must the IEP include all special education and related services*
   needed by the child or only those available from the public agency?

Each public agency must provide a free appropriate public education to all
handicapped children under its jurisdiction. Therefore, the IEP for a handicapped child must include all of the specific special education and related services needed by the child—as determined by the child's current evaluation. This
means that the services must be listed in the IEP even if they are not directly
available from the local agency, and must be provided by the agency through
contract or other arrangements.

45. *Is the IEP a commitment to provide services—i.e., must a public*
   agency provide all of the services listed in the IEP?

Yes. Each handicapped child's IEP must include all services necessary to
meet the child's identified special education and related service needs; and all
services in the IEP must be provided in order for the agency to be in compliance with the Act.

46. *Must the public agency itself directly provide the services set out in*
   the IEP?

The public agency responsible for the education of a handicapped child could
provide IEP services to the child: (1) directly, through the agency's own staff
resources, or (2) indirectly, by contracting with another public or private
agency, or through other arrangements. In providing the services, the agency
may use whatever State, local, Federal, and private sources of support are
available for those purposes (see Sec. 300.301(a)). However, the services
must be at no cost to the parents, and responsibility for ensuring that the IEP
services are provided remains with the public agency.

48. *If modifications are necessary for a handicapped child to participate*
   in a regular education program, must they be included in the IEP?

Yes. If modifications (i.e., supplementary aids and services) to the regular
education program are necessary to ensure the child's participation in that
program, those modifications must be described in the child's IEP (e.g., for a
hearing impaired child, special seating arrangements or the provision of assignments in writing). This applies to any regular education program in

which the student may participate, including physical education, art, music, and vocational education.

49. *When must physical education (PE) be described or referred to in the IEP?*

Section 300.307(a) provides that "… physical education services, specially designed if necessary, must be made available to every handicapped child receiving a free appropriate public education." The following paragraphs: (1) set out some of the different PE program arrangements for handicapped students, and (2) indicate whether, and to what extent, PE must be described or referred to in an IEP:

a. Regular PE with nonhandicapped students.

If a handicapped student can participate fully in the regular PE program without any special modifications to compensate for the student's handicap, it would not be necessary to describe or refer to PE in the IEP. On the other hand, if some modifications to the regular PE program are necessary for the student to be able to participate in that program, those modifications must be described in the IEP.

b. Specially designed PE.

If a handicapped student needs a specially designed PE program, that program must be addressed in all applicable areas of the IEP (e.g., present levels of educational performance, goals and objectives, and services to be provided). However, these statements would not have to be presented in any more detail than the other special education services included in the student's IEP.

c. PE in separate facilities.

If a handicapped student is educated in a separate facility, the PE program for that student must be described or referred to in the IEP. However, the kind and amount of information to be included in the IEP would depend upon the physical-motor needs of the student and the type of PE program that is to be provided.

Thus, if a student is in a separate facility that has a standard PE program (e.g., a residential school for the deaf), and if it is determined—on the basis of the student's most recent evaluation—that the student is able to participate in that program without any modifications, then the IEP need only note such participation. On the other hand, if special modifications to the PE program are needed for the student to participate, those modifications must be described in the IEP. Moreover, if the student needs an individually designed PE program, that program must be addressed under all applicable parts of the IEP. (See paragraph "b," above.)

50. *If a handicapped student is to receive vocational education, must it be described or referred to in the student's IEP?*

The answer depends upon the kind of vocational education program to be provided. If a handicapped student is able to participate in the regular vocational education program without any modifications to compensate for the student's handicap, it would not be necessary to include vocational education in the student's IEP. On the other hand, if modifications to the regular vocational education program are necessary in order for the student to participate in that program, those modifications must be included in the IEP. Moreover, if the student needs a specially designed vocational education program, then vocational education must be described in all applicable areas of the student's IEP (e.g., present levels of educational performance, goals and objectives, and specific services to be provided). However, these statements would not have to be presented in any more detail than the other special education services included in the IEP.

Note: Regulations under the Vocational Education Act provide that: (1) certain funds available under that Act for vocational programs for handicapped persons must be used in a manner consistent with the State's plan under EHA-B, and (2) the five-year State Vocational Education Plan "... shall describe how the program provided each handicapped child will be planned and coordinated in conformity with and as a part of the child's individualized education program as required by the Education of the Handicapped Act." (See 34 CFR 400.141(f)(10), 400.182(f) (formerly 45 CFR 104.141(f)(10), 104.182(f)).)

54. *Must the evaluation procedures and schedules be included as a separate item in the IEP?*

No. The evaluation procedures and schedules need not be included as a separate item in the IEP, but they must be presented in a recognizable form and be clearly linked to the short-term objectives.

Note: In many instances, these components are incorporated directly into the objectives.

56. *Is there a prescribed format or length for an IEP?*

No. The format and length of an IEP are matters left to the discretion of State and local agencies. The IEP should be as long as necessary to adequately describe a child's program. However, as indicated in Question 41, above, the IEP is not intended to be a detailed instructional plan. The Federal IEP requirements can usually be met in a one-to three-page form.

Note: In a national survey conducted under contract with the Department, it was found that 47% of the IEPs reviewed were three pages or less in length.

58. *What provisions on confidentiality of information apply to IEPs?*

IEPs are subject to the confidentiality provisions of both: (1) EHA-B (Section 617(c) of the Act; Secs. 300.560-300.576 of the regulations), and (2) the Family Educational Rights and Privacy Act ("FERPA"; 20 U.S.C. 1232g). An IEP is an "education record" as that term is used in the FERPA and implementing regulations (34 CFR Part 99) and is, therefore, subject to the same protections as other education records relating to the student.

Note: Under Section 99.31(a) of the FERPA regulations, an educational agency may disclose personally identifiable information from the education records of a student without the written consent of the parents "... if the disclosure is—(1) to other school officials, including teachers, within the educational institution or local educational agency who have been determined by the agency or institution to have legitimate educational interests ..." in that information.

59. *If placement decisions are made at the time the IEP is developed,*
    how can a private school representative attend the meeting?

Generally, a child who requires placement in either a public or private residential school has already been receiving special education, and the parents
and school personnel have often jointly been involved over a prolonged period of time in attempting to find the most appropriate placement for the
child. At some point in this process (e.g., at a meeting where the child's current IEP is being reviewed), the possibility of residential school placement
might be proposed by either the parents or school personnel. If both agree,
then the matter would be explored with the residential school. A subsequent
meeting would then be conducted to finalize the IEP. At this meeting, the
public agency must ensure that a representative of the residential school
either: (1) attends the meeting, or (2) participates through individual or conference telephone calls, or by other means.

60. *Is the IEP a performance contract?*

No. Section 300.349 makes it clear that the IEP is not a performance contract that imposes liability on a teacher or public agency if a handicapped
child does not meet the IEP objectives. While the agency must provide special
education and related services in accordance with each handicapped child's
IEP, the Act does not require that the agency, the teacher, or other persons
be held accountable if the child does not achieve the growth projected in the
written statement.

Model Notice to Parents of Procedural Safeguards

This appendix provides parents of children with disabilities from kindergarten through age 21 an overview of their educational rights, sometimes called notice of Procedural Safeguards. This information will also be of interest to individuals serving as surrogate parents.

Some of the following information is new due to recent changes in the Individuals with Disabilities Education Act (IDEA). The IDEA includes the Procedural Safeguards which follow. This appendix was prepared after the changes in Federal law but before new Federal regulations were written.

Notice of Procedural Safeguards must be given to you when you ask for a copy **and**:

- The first time your child is referred for a special education evaluation;

- Each time an individualized education program (IEP) meeting is scheduled for your child;

- Each time your child is reevaluated;

- If you file a complaint or request a due process hearing;

- If the school district takes disciplinary action involving a change in placement of more than ten days for your child; or

- If the school district places your child in an interim alternative educational set-ting for up to 45 days for certain drug- and/or weapon-related misconduct.

For More Information

Your local school district is the first stop for more information. There are a number of people in the school district who can answer your questions about your child's education. You may contact your child's general or special education teacher or the school principal. You can also contact the special education repre-sentative for your school district or education service district (ESD).

Parental Participation

Your participation is valuable. You will be given opportunities to participate in meet-ings about the identification, evaluation, and educational placement of your child, and other matters relating to your child's free appropriate public education (FAPE). This includes the right to participate in meetings to develop your child's IEP.

Parental Consent

The First Evaluation. The school district must have your informed written con-sent before it can evaluate your child. The school district must inform you about the evaluations to be used with your child.

Reevaluation. The school district must have your informed written consent be-fore reevaluating your child. However, the school district may reevaluate your child without your written consent if the school district can demonstrate that it has taken reasonable measures to obtain your consent and you have not res-ponded. State regulations still require parental consent before giving an intelli-gence or personality test. If you refuse consent, you must clearly inform the appropriate school staff of your refusal, preferably in writing.

Initial Placement in Special Education. You must give your informed written consent before the school district can initially place your child in a special educa-tion program.

Refusal. You can refuse consent for an evaluation, a reevaluation, or the initial placement of your child in special education. The school district may seek to evaluate or place your child in special education through a due process hearing, if it believes it is necessary for your child. You and the school district may agree to first try mediation to resolve your disagreements.

Prior Written Notice

In addition to being a participant in decision making, you have the right to prior written notice from the school district after important decisions are made that affect your child's special education but before those decisions are put into place. These include decisions to:

- Identify your child as a child with a disability, or change your child's eligibility from one disability to another;

- Evaluate or reevaluate your child;

- Develop an IEP for your child, or change your child's IEP; or

- Place your child in a special education program, or change your child's special education placement.

You also have the right to prior written notice from the school district when the district refuses your request to take these actions. Prior written notice must include:

- A description of the action proposed or refused by the school district;

- An explanation of why the action is proposed or refused;

- A description of any other options considered and the reasons why those options were rejected;

- A description of each evaluation procedure, test, record, or report used as a basis for the action proposed or refused;

- A description of any other factors relevant to the action proposed or refused;

- A statement that parents of a child with a disability are protected by the Procedural Safeguards described in the IDEA;

- A copy of the Procedural Safeguards, or information about how you can obtain a copy; and

- Sources for you to contact to obtain help in understanding the Procedural Safeguards.

Prior written notice must be provided in your native language unless it is clearly not feasible to do so.

Reevaluation

A child with an IEP must be reevaluated at least once every three years. If the IEP team determines that no additional data are needed to determine whether your child continues to be eligible for special education, the school district must notify you of that decision and the reasons for it. You still have the right to request an assessment to determine whether your child continues to be eligible. Under these circumstances, the school district is not required to do an assessment of your child unless you request one.

Access to Education Records

You have the right to inspect and review all of your child's education records:

- Without unnecessary delay;

- Before any meeting about your child's IEP;

- Before any due process hearing related to your child; and, in any case,

- Within 45 days of your request.

Requests to look at your child's records should typically be made to the building principal or to the special education administrator for your school district.

Access to your child's education records is required by both the Family Educational Rights and Privacy Act (FERPA) and the IDEA. Your school district likely has a more detailed written policy about school records. This policy should be made available to you upon request.

Independent Educational Evaluations

An independent educational evaluation is an evaluation by a qualified examiner who is not an employee of the school district responsible for a child. You may ask for an independent educational evaluation at school district expense if you disagree with an evaluation completed by the school district.

The school district must respond to your request within a reasonable time. If the school district disagrees, it may request a due process hearing. If the school district shows at a hearing that its evaluation is appropriate, the school district will not have to pay for an independent educational evaluation. You may still arrange for an independent educational evaluation at your own expense.

School districts must maintain a list of public and private agencies qualified to conduct independent educational evaluations. This list is available upon request. Typically, requests for this list should be made to the school district's special education administrator.

The results of independent educational evaluations must be considered by the school district when taking further action regarding a child. These evaluations may be considered as evidence in a due process hearing. A hearing officer may also obtain an independent educational evaluation of your child at school district expense during due process hearing proceedings.

Opportunity to Present Complaints

If you have concerns about your child's special education services, the first step is to talk to your child's regular or special education teacher, the building principal, and/or the school district's special education representative. It helps to deal with concerns when they first arise so steps can be taken as soon as possible to support the working relationship among parents, staff, and children. If your concerns are not resolved, you can take further steps to address them, including mediation, a written complaint to the State Department of Education (SDE), and/or requesting a due process hearing.

Mediation

You may ask the school district to try mediation. Mediation is voluntary—both you and the school staff must agree to try mediation before a mediator will be appointed. A mediator is a person who is trained in strategies to help people come to agreement on difficult issues.

If you have requested a due process hearing, the State Department of Education (SDE) will pay the costs of mediation. Otherwise, the costs of mediation will be paid by the school district.

Written Complaints

If you believe your school district has violated the IDEA, you may file a written complaint with the State Department of Education (SDE). This complaint must describe the problem(s), include your name and contact information, and give specific facts about the problem(s). If you file a written complaint of this type, the SDE must investigate.

Due Process Hearings

A due process hearing is a formal legal proceeding. You may request a due process hearing if you disagree with the identification, evaluation, educational placement, or other aspects relating to your child's free appropriate public education (FAPE).

Your hearing request must include:

- Your child's name and address and the name of the school your child is attending;

- A description of the problem, including specific facts about the problem; and

- Any suggestions you have for solving the problem.

The school district also may request a due process hearing when you refuse consent for evaluation or placement or to demonstrate that the school district has conducted an appropriate evaluation and/or offered a free appropriate public education.

The State Department of Education (SDE) will appoint an impartial hearing officer. A hearing officer cannot be an employee of the SDE or a school district involved in the education or care of your child.

A party to a hearing has certain rights, including:

- The right to bring an attorney who can give you advice;

- The right to bring one or more individuals who have knowledge or training about children with disabilities;

- The right to present evidence and confront, cross-examine, and require witnesses to be present;

- The right to a written, or, at your option, an electronic verbatim record of the hearing; and

- The right to written, or, at your option, electronic findings of fact and decisions.

The final order does not identify you or your child by name. It is a public record.

Disclosure of Evidence Before Hearing. At least five business days before a hearing, you and the school district must disclose to each other all evaluations of your child completed by that date and recommendations based upon those evaluations that are intended to be used at the hearing. A hearing officer may bar any party that fails to comply with this rule from introducing the undisclosed evaluations or recommendations at the hearing without the consent of the other party.

Child's Placement During Proceedings. During the process of hearing and appeal, your child remains in his or her current educational placement. This "stay put" rule applies unless:

- You and the school district agree to another placement;

- Your child is applying for initial admission to a public school and you consent to your child's placement in the public school program; or

- Your child is removed to an interim alternative educational setting by school personnel or a hearing officer.

Civil Actions. A decision by a hearing officer is final except that a losing party can bring a civil action in court within 120 days of the final order. If you file a civil action, the court must:

- Receive the record of the hearing;

- Hear additional evidence at the request of a party;

- Base its decision upon the preponderance of the evidence; and

- Grant such relief as the court determines is appropriate.

Attorney Fees. A court may award reasonable attorney fees to the parents of a child with a disability if you prevail in the action. Under certain circumstances attorney fees may be reduced or denied.

School Discipline and Placement in Interim Alternative Educational Settings

Short-Term

Short-term removals are removals of up to ten school days—either at one time or combined in a school year. School personnel may use short-term removals, including suspension, moving your child to an appropriate interim alternative educational setting, or putting your child in another setting, to the same extent these options would be used with children without disabilities.

Longer Removals

Longer removals include expulsion and suspensions that add up to more than ten days in a school year. School districts cannot take this kind of action for misconduct that is a manifestation of your child's disability. If school staff are considering a longer removal, the district must have an IEP meeting, including you, to make a "manifestation determination." This meeting must take place immediately, if possible, or within ten days of the school district's decision to take this type of disciplinary action.

Manifestation Determination

This is when the IEP team determines whether the misconduct is a manifestation of your child's disability. You will be invited to participate as a member of this team. The IEP team may determine that the behavior was **not** a manifestation if the IEP team:

Reviews all relevant information, including:

- Test results, and any independent educational evaluations;

- Information provided by you;

- Observations of your child; and

- Your child's IEP and placement;

And determines that, in light of the misconduct:

- Your child's IEP and placement were appropriate;

- The special education services, supplementary aids and services, and behavioral intervention strategies were provided as described on your child's IEP;

- Your child's disability did not impair his or her ability to understand the impact and consequences of the misconduct; and

- Your child's disability did not impair his or her ability to control the misconduct.

If the IEP team concludes that the misconduct was **not** a manifestation of your child's disability:

- The school district may take disciplinary action, such as expulsion, in the same manner as it would for children without disabilities;

- If an expulsion hearing is required, the school district must ensure the special education and disciplinary records of your child are provided to the expulsion hearing officer, and

- The school district must continue to provide a free appropriate public education to your child consistent with your child's individual needs and the state's alternative educational requirements.

If you disagree with the IEP team's decision, you can request an expedited due process hearing.

Behavioral Plan

Either before or within ten days of taking a disciplinary action, the school district may be required to have an IEP meeting, including you, to:

- Develop an assessment plan to address the misconduct; or

- If your child has a behavioral intervention plan, to review and modify the plan, as necessary, to address the behavior.

Weapon- and Drug-Related Misconduct

School personnel may move your child to an interim alternative educational setting for 45 days if:

- Your child carries a weapon to school or to a school function; or

- Your child knowingly possesses or uses illegal drugs or sells or solicits the sale of a controlled substance while at school or a school function.

Removal by a Hearing Officer

After considering the appropriateness of the current placement, a hearing officer may move your child to an interim alternative educational setting if:

- Your child would be substantially likely to cause injury to himself or herself or others in the current placement;

- The public agency has made reasonable efforts to minimize the risk of harm in the current placement; and

- The interim alternative educational setting meets the requirements described in the next paragraph.

Interim Alternative Educational Setting

Any interim alternative educational setting must:

- Allow your child to continue to participate in the general curriculum, although in a different setting;

- Allow your child to continue to receive services and modifications, including those described in your child's IEP, to enable your child to meet IEP goals; and

- Include services and modifications designed to address your child's behavior.

The specific interim alternative educational setting must be determined by your child's IEP team, including you.

Children Attending Private Schools

Limitation on Services

Children who are enrolled by their parents in private schools may participate in publicly funded special education and related services. Federal law limits the amount that school districts may spend for these services to a proportionate share of Federal IDEA funds.

Federal law permits special education and related services to be provided at the private school to the extent consistent with state law.

When Reimbursement Is Not Required

Some children with disabilities are enrolled in private schools by their parents. The school district is not required to pay for the cost of education, including special education and related services, of your child at a private school or facility if the school district made a free appropriate public education available to your child and you chose to place your child in a private school or facility.

When Reimbursement May be Required

A court or hearing officer may require the school district to reimburse you for the cost of private school placement made without the consent of or referral by the school district only if:

- Your child received special education and related services under the authority of a public agency before enrolling in the private school; and

- The court or hearing officer finds that, at that time, the school district did not make a free appropriate public education available to your child in a timely manner.

When Reimbursement May be Reduced or Denied

Notice Before Removing Your Child From Public School. The court or hearing officer may reduce or deny reimbursement if you did not inform the school district you were rejecting the placement proposed by the school district and state your concerns and your intent to enroll your child in a private school at public expense.

This notice must be given either:

- At the most recent IEP meeting you attended before removing your child from public school; or

- In writing to the school district at least ten business days before removing your child from public school.

A court or hearing officer may **not** reduce or deny reimbursement if you do not give this notice because:

- You are illiterate and cannot write in English;

- Giving notice would likely result in physical or serious emotional harm to your child;

- The school prevented you from giving notice; or

- You had not received a copy of the Procedural Safeguards or otherwise been informed of this notice requirement.

Evaluation by School District. The court or hearing officer also may reduce or deny reimbursement if you do not make your child available for an evaluation by the school district, providing:

- The school district gave prior written notice of its intent to evaluate or re-evaluate your child;

- The purpose of the evaluation as described in the prior written notice was appropriate and reasonable; and

- The prior written notice was given before your child was removed from the public school.

Unreasonableness. Reimbursement may also be reduced or denied upon a judicial finding that you were unreasonable in your actions.

Note: This appendix was adapted by permission from the Oregon Department of Education pamphlet *Parental Rights For Special Education (K-21)*. Copyright © 1997. All rights reserved.

References

Barsch, R.H. (1968). Perspectives on learning disabilities: The vectors of a new convergence. *Journal of Learning Disabilities*, *1*, 7-23.

Bateman, B.D. (1992). *The essentials of teaching*. Creswell, OR: Otter Ink.

Hehir, T. (1997, November 13). Keynote address to International Dyslexia Association Annual Conference, Minneapolis, MN.

Lovitt, T.C. (1991). *Preventing school dropouts*. Austin, TX: Pro-Ed.

Mager, R.F. (1997). *Preparing instructional objectives* (3rd ed). Atlanta, GA: Center for Effective Performance.

Oregon Department of Education. (1997, September). *Parental rights for special education (K-21)* [pamphlet]. Salem, OR: Author.

Smith, C. & Strick, L. (1997). *Learning disabilities: A to Z*. New York: Free Press.

Sugai, G. & Colvin, G. (1990). From assessment to develoment: Writing behavior IEPs. *The Oregon Conference Monograph*, (pp. 125-179). Eugene, OR: University of Oregon.

Walsh, Anderson, Brown, Schulze, & Aldridge, P.C. (1997). *Positive behavioral strategies and consequences* [handout]. Austin, TX: 6300 La Calma, Suite 200, 512-454-6864.

INDEX